Your Past Has Passed

How to Get From Your Present to Your Potential

Your Past Has Passed

How to Get
From Your Present
to Your Potential

Linda H. Williams

Book Cover design by Cathi Stevenson
www.bookcoverexpress.com

Book Edited by
Amy Todisco
www.GreenLivingNow.com

Interior Design by Rudy Milanovich
rudy@wizardvision.com

ISBN: 978-0-9915377-0-9

Linda H. WILLIAMS
A New Dawn Brings A New Beginning

www.LindaHWilliams.com

What People Are Saying about
Your Past Has Passed

"In *Your Past Has Passed*, Linda Williams shares vulnerably her life experiences to provide you with inspiration, a positive role model, and simple step-by-step exercises to help you create a life you love. It's a must read for women looking for a fresh start." — **Manny Goldman, Co-founder, It's All About Women, and Founder of Real Growth Worldwide**

"In today's crazy and frantic age — with so many unknowns and great uncertainty — *Your Past Has Passed* becomes the comforting voice that lays out a compelling blueprint for living a fulfilled life." — **Keith Leon, Multiple Bestselling Author, Book Publisher, and Book Mentor**

"If the art of living is the ability to use misfortune in a constructive fashion, and Linda has provided a superb example of how this is to be accomplished. *Your Past Has Passed* is an informative book which I will share with family and colleagues." — **Rev. Dr. William Holmes Robinson, Servant†Pastor†Teacher, The Olivet Church**

"*Your Past Has Passed* is an invaluable, compassionate, and spiritual harvest of redemptive insights that will both inspire and challenge the reader. This affirming message of empowerment and restoration is a must read." — **Elder Dr. Lehome' Bliss, The Bliss Center, Paracletos Institute International**

"*Your Past Has Passed* offers an empowering message of hope and restoration. This is a must read for anyone feeling stuck in their life journey. We don't always get to choose what happens in our lives, but we can choose how we respond. Linda offers valuable, practical methods for doing so." — **Janet Daughtry, Co-Founder, Life Breakthrough Academy**

"*Your Past Has Passed,* by Linda H. Williams, proves once again that your 'past' does not equal your future. It reminds me of the quote, 'It's not what happens to you but what you do about it that matters!' Linda is using her story to help you write a new story. You can have whatever you want, if you are willing, so bring your willingness, and start reading this book now!" — **David Boufford, a.k.a. Mr. Positive**

"Linda H. Williams is a woman who has traveled a difficult road to arrive where she is today. The insight and wisdom she's gained through her journey serves as an inspiration to women everywhere. Use Linda's powerful lessons to release the baggage you've been carrying, and create the beautiful life that you deserve." — **Cyndi Joudrey, Publisher and Co-CEO of It's All About Women**

"This book is full of inspiration in easily-swallowed doses. Linda's insight catches your attention, and then she drives her points home powerfully, yet succinctly. I would recommend it to all." — **Patricia Altemus, Executive Director of Clayton County Association Against Family Violence**

"I love that Linda has taken her dream to another level. She didn't just talk about the goals, but she made them a reality in changing her life and sharing her experiences to help others better their life's journey along that sometimes rough road of life to allow them to see the new horizon. Linda's personal experiences and philosophies can help you create your own road map to success." — **Elizabeth "Freddie" Johnson, Retired Insurance Business Owner**

"*Your Past Has Passed* takes a holistic approach to self-development, encouraging you to tap into the physical, mental, and emotional aspects of yourself to make positive changes in your life. My tears are only for the joy that I know you will bring others as they share your journey of healing, love, and happiness..."—**Pamela McCray, CDPE/REO/REPM, Keller Williams Realty**

"I have observed how, in just writing this book, Linda has excelled in getting past her past! Her journey has propelled her into an awesome future, which includes sharing these simple but powerful concepts that will create lasting changes in one's life."—**Crystal Barrett, Project Management, The Olivet Church**

"Linda's experiences catch your attention and make you want to read more. Her insights provide the essentials to unpack the baggage that may be holding you back, and this book offers practical tools to actualize your potential."—**Anita Dabney, Real Estate Professional**

"The difficulties and the promises of life are all contained within the fullness of our personal experience of it. This book presents this powerful message in down-to-earth ways that carry big meaning."—**Philomena Slater, MA, CRC, CCM, ACE, Innovation Technology Associates, Inc. Ergonomic Consultant and Physical Training Innovator**

"I have known Linda all of my life, and during my teen years and early adulthood, she was someone I looked up to and held in high esteem. I witnessed her descent to her darker days, and to see how and where she has lifted herself is astounding. Her words of encouragement and plan of action are not just platitudes, but she is living proof of their validity. Congratulations and blessings to you, Linda, as I continue to hold you as a mentor and role model in my life!"—**Rae-Myra Hilliard, Professional Classical Voice Instructor**

"*Your Past Has Passed* is a must read for all women who could use support in going from where they are to where they want to be."— **Rev Clifton Dawkins, Chaplain, Fulton County, GA**

Dedication

This book is dedicated to my mom, who never stopped believing in me, even when I didn't believe in myself and to my dad, who saw this book thirty years ago. I LOVE YOU BOTH.

Rev. and Mrs. John T. Hilliard
Buffalo, New York

Acknowledgements

Thank God, who chose me to show His wondrous redemptive powers.

Thanks to the women of Olivet for their unwavering support from the beginning of my ministry.

Thanks to the late Dr. Howard W. Creecy, Jr., who prayed me through the rough times.

Thanks to Rosalyn Peterson, my oldest and dearest friend, who has always encouraged me.

Thanks to Vanessa Austin, who believed in me and saw my vision and my destiny.

Thanks to Keith Leon, who is taking me from my "present to my potential."

Thanks to David Boufford, who came in answer to a prayer.

Thanks to my sons, Emory and Raphael, who loved me through my dark days.

Thanks to my sister, Joyce, who never let go of my hand until I could see the light again for myself.

Table of Contents

Introduction

I've been homeless, a drunk, a victim, a drug dealer, broke, busted, and downright disgusted. Who I am now is a survivor and an achiever. There are a lot of things I don't know, but what I do know is that our past does not define our present nor does it dictate our future.

Is your future being held hostage by your past? Getting past your past can be a tricky thing. Who you are today is a direct result of your past — your triumphs, your mistakes, and your good and bad decisions. It has molded you into the person you've become. If your past is laden with difficult and painful experiences that you can't get past, cutting yourself off might be easier said than done.

Sometimes we can get stuck and begin to believe that our journey has become our destination. If you are stuck in your past, this can lead to an unhappy present and a dismal future. You have baggage, I have baggage, and we all have baggage that we bring with us. It's how we carry that baggage and what we do with it that determines whether it propels us to greater heights or weighs us down.

As I reflect back on my life, my personal journey to self awareness began after twenty years of not really knowing who I was. The person I saw myself as in high school was not the same person other people saw. I saw a skinny girl with long hair and glasses, who longed to be part of "the group." My classmates saw this pretty girl who was confident, popular, and a leader. Consequently, some of my choices sprang from the baggage of low self-esteem that I brought with me, and those were not always the best decisions.

I've been fortunate in that my good days have outweighed my bad days. I don't complain; I rejoice, and I continue to learn life lessons. I want you to know that your situation doesn't define you. You can either change your situation or change how you respond to it. As long as you have breath, you can grow and develop into the person you want to be.

In this first of a series of books on your personal journey, we give you step- by-step instructions to help you plot your course. So grab a cup of your favorite beverage, and let's take a journey together and explore the process of getting past your past.

The purpose of this book is to help you work through your thoughts and ideas in order to develop a plan of action so that you can begin to formulate the direction you will take to get on the path toward your future. We all have baggage that we bring with us in to the present. Some of it is good, and some of it is not so good. The key to a successful, happy life is to put all of our past into its proper perspective. Everyone, no matter what their past has been, can relate to the emotions, thoughts, and feelings expressed in this book.

The study guide at the end of each chapter will help you to sort out, as well as write out, some of those pieces of baggage that you've been carrying around. If not properly let go, your hurtful past can surface subconsciously and sabotage your future. Since you are the only person who can determine what baggage you carry around, it's important to understand what that baggage is and what steps you need to take to get rid of it. Be honest in your answers. At the end of the day, the whole purpose of this is self-help.

Letting Go Of Guilt

By Kathleen O'Brien

Let go.....
of guilt; it's okay to make the same mistakes again.

Let go....
of obsessions; they seldom turn out the way you planned.

Let go....
of hate; it's a waste of love.

Let go....
of blaming others; you are responsible for your own destiny.

Let go....
of fantasies; so reality can come true.

Let go....
of self-pity; someone else may need you.

Let go....
of wanting; cherish what you have.

Let go....
of fear; it's a waste of faith.

Let go....
of despair; change comes from acceptance and forgiveness.

Let go....
of the past; the future is here ~ right now.

Good Riddance to Guilt

How often have you convicted yourself of a crime that you didn't commit or felt responsible for a situation in which you couldn't change the outcome? Guilt is a normal emotional signal that we learn early in our childhood development. Its purpose is to warn us when we've done something wrong, and to help us see how our behavior impacts ourselves and others around us. It is not meant to be a club with which we constantly beat ourselves up. It should lead us to examine our decisions so that we don't continue to make the same mistakes. We have to learn how to deal with our guilty feelings — to either accept them when they are important, or let them go when they're not. In order to do that, we have to recognize what type of guilt we are dealing with.

Healthy guilt is our conscience telling us that we have done something against our morals and beliefs. It's that little voice that says, "You know you shouldn't have been there in the first place." or "Why did you do that?" This type of guilt should encourage you to take appropriate actions to rectify the situation. This is part of the process of self evaluation in the light of honesty. It requires us to take a long, hard look at ourselves and admit that we may have made a bad decision. It further requires us to take responsibility for our actions. For this type of "healthy guilt," we need to identify and correct the situation to the best of our ability. We must accept responsibility for our actions, ask for forgiveness, and live with the consequences. Even healthy guilt can be dangerous if we don't process this emotion and release ourselves from the angst that results from the consequences.

Unhealthy guilt happens when you feel that everything is your fault — even when you didn't do anything wrong. Sometimes things are totally beyond your control, yet somehow you feel responsible. Blaming ourselves for our children's decisions is a perfect example of unhealthy guilt. Of course we want everything to be perfect in their lives. But when they become adults, we cannot feel responsible for the decisions that they make. If they make a mistake, it is their responsibility, not ours.

Taking the blame for other people's choices can result in low self-esteem. We equate our worthiness with the successes and failures of others. We are not helping others who are at fault by covering for them. We have to learn how to build our confidence and self-worth, and that cannot be contingent upon someone else. We cannot control another person. We have to learn to identify what we can and cannot control, and then let it go. Lingering guilt adds to our mental junk drawer!

False guilt occurs with people who see themselves as victims. People who have experienced abuse or violent crime sometimes feel that it was their fault, and often accept the blame. This is not only false guilt, but it is unhealthy and can lead to other serious consequences. People who have self-destructive behavior patterns often deal with issues of false guilt. They perpetuate the victim syndrome because they are overcome with fear of making the wrong decisions, so they allow someone else to make decisions for them. They have a tendency to rely on someone else's beliefs and comments.

It's imperative that you identify your true feelings and cope with what has happened to keep false guilt from misleading you. Concentrating on things that you cannot control or change only allows false guilt to consume you. Guilt can be emotionally paralyzing, making it difficult for you to move past the thing that caused you the guilt in the first place. You have to use the experience and the associated guilt as a catalyst to action. The road to self-discovery allows you to deal with guilt in a healthy manner. It also limits your vulnerability to other people playing on your feelings of guilt and shame.

People will use your weakness to their advantage. Let's look at ways people use guilt:

1. People will make requests of you and then make you think that they will suffer if you don't do what they ask. You will end up accepting responsibility for someone else's problems or misfortunes, because it will bother you to see them suffer. Ultimately, you will end up doing something that someone else wants you to do— something that makes them happy but makes you unhappy. They will call on your guilt or shame to do what they want, even if it violates your rights. That's called victimization.

2. People will reinforce your negative, irrational thinking by forcing you to have a sense of blame for past, present, and future actions. This can cause regret for any real or imagined misdeeds. Often these actions are beyond your control, yet if you are not careful, people will try to force total responsibility upon you for their misfortune. It amazes me how people who don't take responsibility for their own actions will be quick to point out to someone else how it's their fault that something bad happened. If we are truthful with ourselves, we will see how our own actions result in the consequences of our behavior.

3. People will verbally assault you by creating an environment where you feel that you are at fault even when there has been no action on your part. This will make you think that you have to do anything to alleviate the situation, thus causing you to make an unhealthy decision which further guarantees your sense of shame and guilt. Now you are in a vicious cycle of blame and guilt, further reinforcing your negative self-perceptions. When you have a negative self-image, you allow yourself to be swayed by another person's agenda. This sets the stage for you to be shame ridden, guilt ridden, and self-judgmental for the benefit of someone else.

4. People will threaten negative consequences, often to

themselves, to manipulate your guilt and shame. This will cause you to make decisions to accommodate the manipulator at your expense. Once again, this plays on your negative self-image, which further inhibits your ability to make good decisions. After a while, you will be unable to make any decisions for fear that you may make a wrong one. You begin a pattern of denying yourself, believing that it's actually better to serve others than yourself.

When we live with guilt for a long time, it can feel like all of our thoughts come from guilt. We lose our ability to accept life and all of its blessings. Guilt lingers and becomes toxic to the point where we actually choose to feel guilty in order to maintain a sense of balance. The emotion becomes stagnant and unresolved, dwelling on past mistakes and bad decisions.

We need to understand how this toxic guilt can affect us. Toxic guilt can mask itself as another emotion. It can mask itself as anger about something you specifically did in the past, and you're carrying this around with you today. Your guilt can make you believe you don't deserve to be happy. In addition to anger, there is a sense of something missing in your life that you can't seem to identify. Guilt can also drive you to the point of failed perfection. This type of toxic guilt manifests itself in feelings that if you had tried harder or known more, the outcome would have been different. No matter what you did, it wasn't good enough.

Healing from past guilt requires forgiveness, and letting go of what once was, in order to enjoy the fullness of right now. How do we get past the guilt of our past? We have to learn how to manage our guilt.

Recognize and identify your feelings of guilt.

You have to deal with the reason for your guilt. Once you

determine why you're feeling guilty, you can begin to move forward to release yourself from these feelings. This can be a painful process. It may require you to go back to a painful part of your past and deal with some raw emotions. Sometimes your guilt can be tied to a specific person or situation, but sometimes it's not. Healing is still available from the accompanying symptoms and self-recriminations.

You may find that your guilty feelings are coming from a need to please yourself. Whether it's eating, smoking, drinking, sex, or whatever brings you pleasure, if you feel it is wrong, it will bring on a sense of guilt. Have you broken your code of ethics? Although your feeling of guilt may be healthy, if you allow it to cripple you, you will not derive any benefit from the experience, especially if you cannot change it.

Have you hurt someone, either intentionally or unintentionally? Unless you can do something to rectify that situation, there is little or no value in shouldering that guilt. It is unlikely that you intentionally meant harm; otherwise, you wouldn't be feeling guilty. Sometimes we have to judge ourselves on the motive and not the outcome. Recognize this, and understand the why.

It is only when you can identify the cause of your guilty feelings that you can reconcile yourself. Is your guilt healthy, unhealthy, or false?

Acknowledge your role in the wrongdoing to yourself or others.

As mature adults, we have to accept a certain amount of responsibility for some situations. Have you examined yourself to see what your role was? By not acknowledging that, you perpetuate the guilty feelings you may be having.

Accepting responsibility for your actions and your life is one of the most important aspects of personal development. Anyone can graciously accept success and good times. It takes strong character to successfully cope with adversities and failures and still move forward with a positive outlook—and isn't that the type of person we all want to be? You have to be accountable.

Is the guilt that you're feeling a result of something you did that hurt someone else? Was it your fault? Could the entire situation have been avoided if you had acted differently? Would the outcome have changed? These are questions that must be answered to truly get a clear picture of your role.

Are you so busy blaming someone else that you can't even see your role? Often we get so fixated on pointing the finger at someone else that we totally remove ourselves and our accountability from the situation. Can you be truthful about what happened? We can lie to ourselves so much that in our minds it becomes our reality. It is only when we are truthful to ourselves and others that we can hope to change our behavior for a better tomorrow. We have to acknowledge our strengths and our weaknesses.

Doing the right thing, in every situation, is hard to do and also hard to always keep in mind. So don't aim for perfection; just try to be as good a person as you can be right now

Are you getting any positive experiences from feeling guilty?

- Guilt demonstrates that you have a conscience.

- Are you channeling your guilt into making better relationships?

- Are you using your guilt to recognize when you have said or done something hurtful and taking that opportunity to rectify the situation?

- Can you recognize this feeling of guilt in someone else?

- Can you empathize with this person and try to help them overcome their guilty feelings?

- Have you taken the opportunity to say you're sorry?

- Have you taken the opportunity to make amends for any wrong doing?

- Has your guilt provoked a change in your attitude?

- Have you changed your thinking from negative to positive?

- Are you allowing your guilt to motivate you to be sensitive to someone else's issues?

- Are you helping other people with their issues of guilt?

Seek forgiveness.
(This includes forgiving yourself.)

Forgiving ourselves is essential for healing. Sometimes our guilt makes us feel as though we are unforgiveable. To begin this self-forgiveness process, you have to look back on each experience in your past where you are still carrying guilt or shame. Look at what your true intention was when you did what you did. If you look deeply enough, you may discover that your truest intention was not to hurt someone else, but to take care of yourself in the best way you knew how at the time. You may have had a limited awareness of options. Perhaps you made choices that brought you and others undesirable results, but you did the best you could at the time.

You need to see the truth of this for yourself—that all of your actions came from a basic human survival instinct which, in essence, is to love yourself. If your guilt is for a specific and rational purpose, then it's healthy guilt, so take action to fix the problem behavior. While many of us are gluttons for self-punishment, ongoing guilt weighs us down as we try to move forward in life. It's easy enough to apologize to someone whom we've offended by a careless remark. It's a little more challenging to not only recognize how your behavior may be harming your family, but also to make a change. Healthy guilt tells us that we need to do something differently in order to repair relationships that are important to us.

Learn from the situation so you don't repeat the same mistakes.

Guilt's purpose isn't to make you feel bad just for the heck of it. The feeling of guilt is trying to get your attention so that you can learn something from the experience. If you learn from your behavior, you will be less likely to repeat it in the future. If I've accidentally said something insulting to another person, my guilt is telling me I should: a) apologize to the person or b) think a little more before I speak.

While sometimes we already know the lesson that guilt is trying to teach us, it will return time and time again until we've actually learned the lesson fully. It can be frustrating, but it seems to be the way guilt works for most people. The sooner we learn the lesson (e.g., make amends, work to not engage in the same hurtful behavior in the future, etc.) the sooner the guilt will disappear. If we are successful, guilt will never return for that issue again.

If your guilt isn't trying to correct an actual mistake you made in your behavior, then there's not a whole lot you need to learn. Instead of learning how to change that behavior, you can instead try to understand why a simple behavior most people wouldn't feel guilty about is making you feel guilty.

Let go of the past and move on.

Letting go of your past means accepting that there's nothing more you can do to change the past. You did the best you could.

When you're looking back at your past decisions or actions, know that you were as good, loving, and effective as you could have been. If you were to go back, you couldn't do anything differently, because that's who you were and that's what you knew then. It's done. Let go of your past.

If you did something wrong or hurtful, you will have to accept that you cannot change the past. But you can make amends for your behavior if and when it's appropriate. Do so, apologize, or make up for the inappropriate behavior in a timely manner. Then let it go. The more we focus on believing that we need to do something more, the more it will continue to bother us and interfere with our relationships with others.

Guilt is usually very situational. That means we get into a situation, we do something inappropriate or hurtful, and then we feel badly for a time. Either the behavior wasn't so bad and/or time passes, and we feel less guilty. If we recognize the problem behavior and take action sooner rather than later, we'll feel better about things (and so will the other person), and the guilt will be alleviated. Obsessing about it and not making any type of compensatory behavior (such as apologizing or changing one's negative behavior) keeps the bad feelings going. Accept and acknowledge the inappropriate behavior, make your amends, and then move on.

How do you heal and move past the guilt?

- Realize you can't change the past. Eliminate the "should've, could've, would've" from your vocabulary. Yesterday is gone, today is here, and tomorrow is hoped for.

- Disrupt thoughts of guilt by distraction or by thinking or saying "STOP!"

- If you believe in God or a higher power, consider what He or She has to say about forgiveness.

- Participate in an appropriate support group.

- Be your own best friend. What would you say to your best friend if this had happened to that person? Can you say the same to yourself?

- Remember the good things you did in your relationship and all the loving care you gave. Write those things down, hold onto them, and read them when you need to.

- Channel your guilt into a worthwhile project. If you've learned a lesson from this loss, you may want to share your newfound knowledge with others.

Guilt is one of those emotions that we feel is telling us something important. Be aware that not every emotion, and certainly not every guilty feeling, is a rational one that has a purpose. Focus on the guilt that causes loved ones or friends harm. Remember to be skeptical the next time you feel guilty. Is it trying to teach you something rational and helpful about your behavior, or is it just an emotional, irrational response to a situation? The answer to that question will be your first step in helping you better cope with guilt in the future.

Nobody is perfect, not even your friends and family members who appear to lead perfect, guilt-free lives. Striving for perfection in any part of your life is a recipe for failure, since it can never be attained.

We all make mistakes, and many of us go down a path in our lives that can make us feel guilty later on when we finally realize our mistake. The key, however, is to realize the mistake and accept that you're only human. Don't engage in days, weeks, or months of self-blame or battering your self-esteem because you should've known, should've acted differently, or should've been an ideal person. You're not, and neither am I. That's just life.

Guilt is a normal emotional signal that we learn early in our childhood development. Its purpose is to warn us when we've done something wrong and to help us see how our behavior impacts ourselves and others around us.

Healthy Guilt: Tells you when you've done something against your moral beliefs

1. Identify your morals. What do you believe in? Prioritize the following list in order of importance to you, with 1 being the most important.

Honesty _____   Integrity _____   Compassion _____

Courage _____   Civic Duty _____   Self-Control _____

Fairness _____   Persistence _____   Empathy _____

Diligence _____   Peace _____   Patience _____

Forgiveness _____   Loyalty _____   Self-Respect _____

Competitiveness _____   Respect for Others _____

2. Be honest with yourself. Which of the above morals make you feel guilty and why?

_____

_____

_____

_____

_____

_____

3. What were the consequences of your actions?

_____

_____

_____

_____

_____

_____

_____

4. Can you correct the situation? If so, how?

_____

_____

_____

_____

_____

_____

_____

Unhealthy Guilt: Do you feel that everything is your fault?

1. Who in your life makes you, or has made you, feel guilty?

_____

_____

_____

_____

_____

_____

2. How do/did they make you feel as if it's your fault?

_____

_____

_____

_____

_____

_____

3. Why do you feel it's your fault?

_____

_____

_____

_____

_____

_____

_____

4. What can you do to change the situation?

_____

_____

_____

_____

_____

_____

_____

False Guilt: Do you think of yourself as a victim?

1. Have you experienced abuse or a violent crime?

_____

_____

_____

_____

_____

_____

2. How was that situation your fault?

_____

_____

_____

_____

_____

_____

3. What could you have done to prevent it?

_____

_____

_____

_____

_____

_____

4. What can you do now to change what happened?

_____

_____

_____

_____

_____

_____

5. What decisions are you allowing someone else to make for you?

_____

_____

_____

_____

_____

_____

Guilt as a Weakness

1. How can people use your guilt to their advantage?

_____

_____

_____

_____

_____

_____

2. What do you do that allows this to happen?

_____

_____

_____

_____

_____

_____

_____

3. What can you do to change this pattern?

_____

_____

_____

_____

_____

_____

_____

4. How will that change make your life different?

_____

_____

_____

_____

_____

_____

_____

Healing From Your Guilt

1. How are you channeling your guilt into better
   relationships?

_____

_____

_____

_____

_____

_____

_____

2. How can you use your guilt to change your attitude?

_____

_____

_____

_____

_____

_____

3. What can you learn from your "guilt of the past" so that you don't make the same mistake(s) again?

_____

_____

_____

_____

_____

_____

_____

_____

4. How can you use your guilt to help someone else with their issues of guilt?

_____

_____

_____

_____

_____

_____

5. What can you do to move past your guilt?

_____

_____

_____

_____

_____

_____

_____

Our Choices

Author Unknown

The choices we make are like seeds we plant
along the way.

It's fruit of what we've chosen
that we harvest every day.

Be careful then what you choose,
for in your garden it will grow.

Our choices will produce
the bounty that will show.

The choices you've made,
whether good or bad,

Have set the pace for what you've faced
and the results that you've had.

There may be times when you'll suffer
for poor choices of the past,

But your choice to serve Jesus will be one that lasts.

Personal Choices

What was the first decision that you made today? *Should I hit the snooze button, again? What am I going to wear to work? What am I going to do with my hair?* We make choices every waking minute of our lives. From the minute we open our eyes in the morning until we close them at night, we make hundreds of decisions that impact our day and ultimately, our lives. For those who are confident, decisions are made based on fact. But when life has not gone the way we wanted it to, we can become fearful of making the wrong decision, so we don't make any decision at all. Unfortunately, no decision is actually a decision in and of itself—and probably not the one in our best interest.

There are times when most of us wish we could go back and make a better choice. Yesterday is gone. Though we can't change yesterday's choices, we can change how we allow those choices to influence our decisions today. If we concentrate on what "could've, would've, should've" been, we'll miss opportunities for a better tomorrow.

Have you ever wondered: *How did I get myself into this mess?* This mess is the consequence of a choice you made, and we must live with those consequences. So, if your life isn't exactly what you thought it would be, you may need to take a look at some of the choices that you made along the way. If you don't want your life to continue the way it is, you are going to have to change the choices you make. Where we are today is in direct correlation to the choices we've made.

When we allow people, situations, or circumstances to influence our choices, the consequences are often not what we want. A young girl gets angry at her parents for a house rule and makes the decision to run away. She could end up in a much worse situation than any house rule her parents made! Let's say a woman receives a humiliating comment about her appearance from someone she trusts. She then looks in the mirror and doesn't like what she sees, so she starts altering her body. Pretty soon, it becomes difficult to find the real her. These are examples of choices we make because of an external influence, and then we have to deal with the consequences.

When I look back over my life, I can see where I made some choices based on my situation at the moment, and other people's expectations, and not on personal life goals. That happens a lot to us. We make choices that are not in our best interest. We have to live with the consequences of those choices. Choices that are made without conscious consideration of what the results might be lead us to where we are today. So again, if we are not where we want to be today, we have to look at some of the choices that we made yesterday that got us to where we are today.

Sometimes we allow bitterness and blame to cloud our understanding of our current situation. When that happens, we lose our ability to be able to make good, sound decisions. It is very easy to blame someone else for the decisions we've made that have landed us in the situation we're in today. It is a normal thing to blame someone else. We tell ourselves that it was not our fault. That's what we used to say as children, and we continue to say the same thing as adults. We land in certain situations based on choices that we made, and when it doesn't work out like we thought it would, we immediately blame someone else for our dilemma.

We don't have to accept and allow failure and anger to control our lives. If we recognize that we made the choices that got us to this point, and we accept that our goal was not consistent with the choices we made, then we can more effectively evaluate where we are and where we want to go.

We must deal with consequences of choices that we've made. God gave us all the right to make decisions, and we've got to understand that our personal choices affect our lives. Sometimes we look at our life and wonder what happened. What did we do to get ourselves in this situation? Somewhere along the road, we made choices, and what we're living today is the consequences of those choices. Fortunately, each and every day that the Lord gives us, we get an opportunity to make more choices. The choices we made yesterday landed us where we are today. Which means where we land tomorrow will be a direct reflection of the choices we make today.

If you listen to older people, some of them are so bitter about the choices they made that they shouldn't have, or the choices that they decided not to follow through on. We carry around a lot of baggage from the past. I call it a mental junk drawer. You know that drawer that everyone has in their kitchen or bathroom? It's the one that you put stuff in that you don't know what to do with, but you don't want to throw it away, because you might need it someday. We also do that mentally. We have thoughts, actions, and choices from the past that we are not letting go of. We don't really know what to do with these things, but we don't want to let them go. So, we stick them in our mental junk drawer. And just like with that junk drawer in your kitchen where you stick your hand in and fumble around, you inevitably hurt yourself on a sharp object. That's what happens with our mental junk drawer. We go around picking through the mental junk to see what we can find. Often, we run across an old choice or decision that we made that didn't turn out quite like we expected it to, and we experience that hurt all over again. We still haven't come to grips with exactly what our role was in that decision-making process. We may still be blaming another person. A lot of people don't want to be responsible for the choices that they make. They don't want to admit that their decisions had real life consequences.

When my boys were little (around the age of five), I taught them that if they made a bad choice and stole a piece of candy, the consequence of that decision would be a spanking. If you make that same choice at age fifteen, twenty-five, or even fifty-five, the consequences of that decision will have greater implications and consequences. As much as we might try, we cannot escape the consequences of our choices.

Whether it was a good or bad decision, we must pay the consequences. People think they can make a bad decision and escape the consequences. We see that all the time in the news. Violence has run rampant in our society, and it seems as though the perpetrators don't even give a second thought to the consequences. There was a case where three young men decided to rob a store to get money to celebrate the birthday of one of them. In the process of the robbery, they shot and killed the store clerk. That was a bad decision that not only affected the rest of their lives, but also the lives of the victim's family.

We can use our freedom to choose the path in life that we want. We have to do that by making the right decisions. Bad choices lead to bad consequences. We do reap what we sow. There is great power within us to be able to make good choices in life. We have a choice in terms of what kind of life we want to live. If we are not living the type of life we want to live, we have a choice. We can continue to live that life or we can make a decision to change the life we're living.

When we are responsible and accountable for our own lives and for the decisions we make, we can change our lives for the better. We can make a choice to be happy, and we can make a decision to react positively to all our life's situations. I wake up daily with the intention of being happy and having a good day. That's what living your life on purpose is about. What have you decided for yourself?

That is not to say that things, people, and situations don't happen that send us off base. The scripture does not tell us that we will live a life free from worry and pitfalls. What it does say is that we've got somebody that's here to help comfort us in those situations and give us the strength to get back up again. We will all have challenges in life. That's what life is—a drama.

Every day, every one of us makes choices. We make a choice first thing in the morning when the alarm goes off. Am I going to get up, or am I going to hit the snooze button? If we hit that snooze button too many times, the consequence is that we oversleep and have to rush to get to work on time. This could lead to a very costly speeding ticket, which probably is not a good choice. We must understand that choices are influenced by many factors. We have obligations and responsibilities, and every decision that we make has a great effect on our lives and the lives of other people.

The simplest decisions that we make are the ones that are usually only based on our own needs and wants—those choices that don't impact anybody else. More often than not, the choices that we make are going to impact other people. If we have children, spouses, and family, we cannot make selfish decisions based purely on our own wants and needs. We've got to understand the impact. Is a decision that is based on our own needs, but hurts other people, the right choice? Or, is making a choice that benefits others, but hurts us the wrong choice? Sometimes we have to consider the consequences of making a decision that's in only our best interest or in the best interest of someone else.

Let's look at a woman in an abusive relationship. If she makes the decision to leave but has not looked at the consequences of that decision, she and her children may end up homeless and hungry. Her choice to leave may be in her immediate best interest to escape the abuse, but is it also in the best interest of her children?

Now I'm not advocating that anyone stay in an abusive relationship. What I am saying is that before deciding to leave, we need to be aware of and prepared to deal with the consequences of that choice. So, if we know a woman in an abusive situation, we cannot judge her negatively because of her decision to stay. We don't know everything that's going on in her life. Those of us with children know that there are times when we may sacrifice ourselves for the best interest of our children. That's what we do. If I were in an abusive relationship and I had children and didn't know how I was going to feed them or where they were going to sleep at night, my decision might be to stay for the sake of my children. We cannot judge another person's decision just because we do not agree with it. We don't know everything that has gone into making that decision. Who among us is fit to judge the validity of someone else's choice? None of us are, because none of us have to live with the consequences of that decision.

I would suggest that each of us look at the choices and decisions we make that personally affect our lives. We have to search within ourselves to see whether we are taking responsibility for those choices or blaming someone else. We cannot say what we would or would not do in someone else's life until we have been in that situation. It has been said, "Don't judge a man until you have walked a mile in his shoes." We cannot say that we would not stay in an unhealthy relationship and be treated badly until we are faced with that situation. We have to make a decision, at that point, as to what we should do.

We have to be careful about the choices that we make. All of us can hope for the freedom to make our own choices and the wisdom to learn from those experiences, and for the people who are in our lives to love us enough to respect our decisions. The choice is ultimately ours, and if we continue to make bad decisions, we will continue to get bad results. You cannot expect a different outcome if you keep doing the same thing. So, if you're making the same bad choices, getting the same results, and wondering why your situation hasn't changed, you've got to look at the decisions you're making.

If you are stuck in the middle of an unhappy situation or relationship, how often do you feel that you don't have a choice? No matter where you are in life, there is always a choice that you can make to proceed. We cannot change what happened yesterday; yesterday is gone. We can change what is going on today, which will ultimately affect our tomorrow.

Life is filled with infinite choices. It is up to us to decide the best action for us, based on where our hearts are. If our hearts are aligned with the will of the Lord, He will help us through the Holy Spirit, which is here to lead and guide us. We need to make decisions based on His will for our lives. The scripture says that He will give us the desires of our hearts. That is true, but our hearts have to be in alignment with His will. We cannot choose to do something outside of the will of the Lord and expect a good outcome. We have to understand that it is up to us to decide the best action. This means that we have the ability to choose what we no longer wish to experience. We can also choose what we do want to experience in life. Recognizing that we do have the will and the ability to be able to choose is rewarding, and we will be rewarded for making right choices.

Often, we live our lives without even making a conscious choice. We tend to get to the point where we accept the circumstances of our lives and anything that comes our way. This is the way it is. And why is that? Because that is the way it's always been. We never challenge why it is this way! Sometimes we say that these are generational curses.

We've got to get to the point where we stop blaming what happened yesterday for our current situation and the choices we're making today. When we wake up in the morning, we either are or are not living the life God intended for us to live. We are wonderfully and beautifully made in His image. We've got to convince ourselves that we have the ability to choose a different path in life. So, if where you are now is not where you want to be, are you willing to make the choice to change?

In order to be happy we must accept responsibility for ourselves. We cannot depend on someone else to make us happy. That is a bad choice, because if that person leaves, they take our happiness with them. Then we are left wondering what happened. Yesterday, we thought everything was going along well, and then all of a sudden, the rug gets pulled out from under us, and we're miserable.

We've got to realize that all that we need to be truly happy and fully complete is already within us. Being happy comes from learning about ourselves and our full potential in life—living our lives on purpose. We've got to retrain our brains. Sometimes we get so focused on the negative part of a situation that we don't see the whole picture. We've got to develop a better attitude, which will lead to the ability to make better choices, which will lead to more positive and beneficial consequences.

Life is filled with choices, and you're bound to make some bad ones. Just like parenting your first child, life is all about trial and error, and you pray that you survive. It's a terrible feeling when you make a bad decision. It's even worse if you are so fearful of making a wrong decision that you don't make any decision. You have to get past the fact that you may have made a bad choice and begin to unravel the consequences of those choices.

Take Responsibility

1. Think about one bad decision you've made in the past. Write it down.

_____

_____

_____

_____

_____

2. What was the consequence of that decision? How did it impact your life?

———————————————————————

———————————————————————

———————————————————————

———————————————————————

———————————————————————

———————————————————————

3. What excuses did you make for it not being your fault?

———————————————————————

———————————————————————

———————————————————————

———————————————————————

———————————————————————

———————————————————————

———————————————————————

4. What was your role?

_____

_____

_____

_____

_____

_____

_____

Understand the Decision

1. Why did you make that decision?

_____

_____

_____

_____

_____

_____

2. What was going on in your life at the time that influenced your decision?

_____

_____

_____

_____

_____

_____

_____

3. How can you avoid making the same decision again?

_____

_____

_____

_____

_____

_____

_____

4. What can you do to make better decisions?

_____

_____

_____

_____

_____

_____

_____

5. What effect did your decision have on the other people in your life?

_____

_____

_____

_____

_____

_____

_____

Focus on the Present

1. What can you fix or change?

_____

_____

_____

_____

_____

_____

2. What do you need to do to make yourself feel better?

_____

_____

_____

_____

_____

_____

_____

3. What positive things are you doing now that you can focus on?

_____

_____

_____

_____

_____

_____

_____

4. How can you make amends for a decision that hurt someone?

_____

_____

_____

_____

_____

_____

_____

5. Why are you still angry or hurt over that decision?

_____

_____

_____

_____

_____

_____

Be Proactive for the Future.

1. What would you do different if you were in the same situation again?

_____

_____

_____

_____

_____

_____

2. How can you change your circumstances?

_____

_____

_____

_____

_____

_____

3. What can you do to develop a better attitude about your situation?

_____

_____

_____

_____

_____

_____

4. What have you learned?

_____

_____

_____

_____

_____

_____

_____

Accepting Responsibility

Author Unknown

Something I'm learning,
something that I know is true:

The only person responsible for your actions is you.

What goes around comes around,
as you may have heard.

You give and take, you receive what you deserve.

As much as I may not want to admit,
this mess that I'm in,

I got myself into it.

What I've done, I've done a couple of times.

They say you live and learn, well why didn't I?

So I'm dealing with the pain, and taking on the ache.

I have to lie in the bed I didn't mean to make.

So instead of looking up to heaven and asking God
for help,

I'll take a look in the mirror, a good look at myself.

I have to realize and accept what I've done wrong,

Learning lessons is tough, but not if you're strong.

Accepting Responsibility

Accepting responsibility for the actions in our life is probably one of the most important aspects of our personal development. It's fairly easy to be gracious and accept success in good times. It takes a strong character to successfully cope with the adversities of life — the failures that we experience — and still move forward with a positive attitude. That is the type of person that we should strive to be in the face of adversities.

We know that we have a Comforter. He did not say that we wouldn't fall or have bumps in the road. What He did say was that when we fall, we can rest in His arms, as He is our Comforter.

There are also certain things that we have to do for ourselves. We've got to accept personal responsibility for ourselves and our actions. When we accept that responsibility, we acknowledge that we are ultimately responsible for the choices that we make in our lives. We have to accept the consequences of whatever choices we make. We are responsible for how we choose to feel and how we chose to think. It does not matter how someone else treats us; we cannot control that. What we can control is how we respond to that. How we react to and take personal responsibility for those actions, ultimately, will dictate the direction of our lives. If we choose to be negative and have a negative response for the actions and things that happen in our lives, then that is the direction that our lives will go in.

We've got to believe that we determine who we are and how our choices will affect us today and tomorrow. If we continue to blame someone else, we have given that person authority over us. That is not how the Lord wants us to live — with someone having authority over us. If we choose not to accept personal responsibility for our lives, then we have ultimately given that control to someone else.

We've got to realize that as adults, and as we mature in our spiritual growth, we determine the self-esteem that we will develop. Our self-esteem depends largely on how well we accept personal responsibility. Not accepting responsibility for ourselves and our actions will cause us to have low self-esteem. By blaming someone else, we've given that person permission to determine our self-worth. We've got to stop saying that it's not our fault—that we didn't have the best upbringing or that something bad happened to us as a child. These are all excuses that we use to refuse to accept responsibility for ourselves. These things may have happened in our lives, but that was yesterday. If we are still making choices dependent on things that happened yesterday that we cannot go back and change, then we have to accept that responsibility.

We've got to let go of the anger over those things that happened in the past, and toward those people who mistreated us. That anger is now forcing us to make certain decisions—decisions that we are going to have to live with and take responsibility for—that may not be in our best interest. We've got to be accountable. Even if the other person was out of line, we are responsible for ourselves; we cannot control someone else.

Remember when Flip Wilson used to say that the devil made him do it? Well, the devil didn't make you do anything. You made a decision to do whatever it was. Stop blaming the devil. Blaming someone else started back in the Garden of Eden.

Adam told the Lord, "It was that woman you gave me."

Eve said, "It was that snake's fault!"

We choose how we react or respond. So whatever outcome develops from those reactions, we've got to take responsibility for it.

Sometimes it's just a matter of acknowledging what happened. When we acknowledge that we made a mistake, it eliminates the need to make up excuses. That's what happens when we don't accept responsibility. If we have children then we know that from rearing them. When they refuse to accept responsibility for something they've done, they start to make excuses. We can see through that. We do that as adults, but the consequences are greater. By accepting personal responsibility for ourselves and our decisions, we can move through our day with a much more positive attitude.

I'm sure we all know people who refuse to take responsibility for their behavior. They become very negative and cynical. These are the folks that seem to blame other people. They have the worst luck. Well, if you're a child of the King, luck doesn't fit anywhere in your life. Luck and faith do not go hand in hand. God is not a God of luck or chance. So if we are HIS children, then whatever happens to us is not a result of luck. We have been given the right to make choices. Whether good or bad, these choices have consequences that we must take personal responsibility for. If we know who we are and whose we are, then our lives are not contingent upon luck. Luck means that you are depending on something or somebody else to determine your fate in life. By accepting responsibility for your life, you take that control out of the hands of someone else.

When we take responsibility for having the life we want, we switch our focus from what's wrong with our life to everything that is right about our life. That's what accepting personal responsibility is. We've all made mistakes. I've made bad decisions and bad choices. Through the course of time and bad decisions, I lost my home, my car, and my job. At some point, I had to accept that it was not anyone else's fault but my own. I had made the decision that I would depend on someone else to take care of me, and I had stopped taking care of myself. When I got to the point in my life where I could take a long hard look at myself, I had to be accountable, and I had to take responsibility for certain things that happened in my life. When I lost my home, I had blamed someone else, because I had depended on him to pay the mortgage. When he didn't pay, I lost my home. But his name wasn't even on the deed. That was my home and, ultimately, my responsibility.

There are some things that happen in our lives that are not a consequence of a choice we made. We have to understand that in those situations, we must not take ownership of it. There are some things that happen in our lives that we have no control over. And, it is those things that we have no control over — such as becoming single through the death of a spouse — that we should not accept personal responsibility for.

Everything we do has consequences. We must begin to show good judgment and exercise emotional control in any given situation. Getting angry at someone because they're angry at you is not taking control of the situation. When someone asks you why you did something, and you respond that someone else started it, you are not accepting responsibility for your actions.

We've got to learn how to forgive ourselves. If we've made a mistake, it's better to just admit that mistake. That is the beginning of accepting personal responsibility. If we need to apologize, then apologize. Let it go, and move on. When we dwell on the mistakes that we've made in our lives, we only make them more important than they should be. We cannot concentrate on the positive things in our lives if we are hanging on to the mistakes that we've made.

If we feel the need to explain why we did something, then explain it. Don't make excuses. When we don't accept the responsibility for it, we allow ourselves to be backed into a corner where we can become defensive. Then we try to explain or justify ourselves. If we had just accepted responsibility in the first place, we wouldn't have to do that. That's what happens when we succumb to a victim's mentality. We feel that we have no power or control over anything, and that is not the type of women we want to be.

Empowerment has to come from within. We cannot allow anyone to have that level of power over us, except the Lord. That means that we have to accept those things in our lives that we have control over or input in. Accept the mistakes. We might not always be right. If not, admit it, let it go, and move on.

When we don't accept personal responsibility, we become overly dependent on someone else for their affirmation, recognition, and acceptance. That means that we cannot get through the day without having someone comment on how we look, what we've accomplished, etc. If we don't get that praise, then we don't have a good day. We have to rely on other people, thereby giving them the power and control over how we feel about ourselves. That's what happens when we depend on other people for our joy and happiness. If we depend on other people for that, and they decide that they no longer want us to be happy or have joy, they will simply take it away. Then we wonder what happened. We thought everything was fine, and suddenly the rug is swept out from under us.

So what do we have to do to accept responsibility?

1. We have to stop blaming others. If you wanted to, you could make a long list of people you could blame for the less pleasant aspects of your life. If you're honest, you probably have already blamed some of these people. You made choices, and those choices have consequences. No one else is responsible for the choices that we make. So, if you want things to be different, you have to decide to make those necessary changes.

2. Stop making excuses. We are all guilty of making excuses. When those excuses impede your ability to accept responsibility, then you are accepting defeat. That's

when you have allowed someone or something else to control you. We all have situations in our past that we can use as an excuse for where we are now. Making excuses for your past will not change your future.

3. Stop playing the victim. Not accepting responsibility places us in the role of victim. It says: *This is not my fault. Why is this happening to me?* We get in a mentality of "woe is me!" Since we've allowed ourselves to play the victim, we wait for someone to come along and rescue us. When that happens, that just furthers our victim mentality. We have to go from a victim mentality to a survivor to an overcomer. I am not a victim. I will determine my destiny!

4. Be accountable. We have to accept that we are solely responsible for our actions. No matter what the situation is, we ultimately make the choice on how we are going to respond. Even if we don't respond, we've made a decision not to, and therefore have allowed someone else to make that decision for us. We can blame others, make excuses, or whine, but at the end of the day, we have to take some positive steps to change. If there is something going on in your life that you don't like, change it. If something is broke in your life, fix it. Small changes can lead to big results.

5. Take some positive action. You'll never get anywhere in life if you don't start taking steps in the right direction. As I stated, a small step in the right direction will put you in a totally different frame of mind. You'll begin to see that you are doing something to change where you are. Once you begin to see small changes in your life, it will give you the confidence that you need to make some major changes in your life.

We are the sum of all our choices in life. Naturally, things happen to us that are beyond our control, but we still choose how to respond. Our lives become exactly what we make of them. We can either let life beat us up, or we can choose to accept responsibility for our lives, take appropriate action, and live a better life. All of us have been guilty of feeling sorry for ourselves when life dealt us a bad hand, but we have to also realize that our successes have come when we took responsibility for our results and made things happen. Personal responsibility is a choice. To improve our lives, we can and must accept responsibility for them.

The only way to move "past your past" and on to a better life is to accept personal responsibility for your situation and make a conscious decision to make things different. Accepting responsibility is a major step on the road to self-discovery.

General

1. What does accepting personal responsibility mean to you?

_____

_____

_____

_____

_____

_____

_____

2. How can failing to accept personal responsibility result in negative consequences?

_____

_____

_____

_____

_____

_____

_____

3. What do people who have not accepted personal responsibility believe?

_____

_____

_____

_____

_____

_____

4. What behavior traits need to be developed in order to accept personal responsibility?

_____

_____

_____

_____

_____

_____

_____

_____

5. What are the steps in accepting personal responsibility?

_____

_____

_____

_____

_____

_____

_____

6. What are some reasons why people refuse to accept responsibility?

_____

_____

_____

_____

_____

_____

Specific

1. What specific excuses have you used multiple times to avoid taking responsibility for your own condition?

_____

_____

_____

_____

_____

_____

2. What are some things in your life that you can begin to take control of?

_____

_____

_____

_____

_____

_____

3. What are three actions that you can take this week to demonstrate that you are accepting responsibility for your situation?

_____

_____

_____

_____

_____

_____

_____

4. What are some things in your life that are beyond your control?

_____

_____

_____

_____

_____

_____

_____

_____

5. What do you need to do to surrender these things?

_____

_____

_____

_____

_____

_____

_____

Personal

1. What situation in your life do you believe is not your fault?

_____

_____

_____

_____

_____

_____

2. How do you feel about that situation?

_____

_____

_____

_____

_____

_____

3. How did you react to the situation?

_____

_____

_____

_____

_____

_____

4. What did you do to help create the situation?

_____

_____

_____

_____

_____

_____

_____

5. How would you like things to happen the next time?

_____

_____

_____

_____

_____

_____

_____

6. What can you do to affect a better outcome?

_____

_____

_____

_____

_____

_____

_____

Relax — Let Go of Anger

Relax, let go
Let go of your useless worry,
let go of your helpless fury
Let go of your hopeless fears,
let go of your needless tears.

Relax, let go
Let go of the knot in your stomach,
let go of the tightness in your chest
Let go of the tension in your muscles,
let go of the pain in your head.

Relax, be still
Calm your restless breathing,
slow down your ragged heartbeat.
Be still and think peace. Peace, peace be still
Stop your mumbling and moaning,
quit your grumbling and groaning
Of what use is pining and whining,
or muttering and murmuring?

Relax, be still
In the waters of quietness,
you can walk with the Lord
And above all the noisiness you can hear His word

So relax — be still and know that He is God

Dealing With Your Anger

Anger is a normal emotion to feel, just like happiness or sadness. It can even sometimes motivate us into positive action. But when anger is not expressed in a healthy and positive manner, it can lead to all sorts of problems for us, our family members, and anyone that we might be in a relationship with. We all have "stuff" that has happened to us. If we could have dealt our own hand in life, no one would have dealt the hand that they've got. But life is not about playing with a good hand, it's about playing well with the hand that you've got.

We have to learn how to control our anger before it controls us. Anger can be caused by internal or external events. A long debilitating illness, a sudden traffic jam, and you're already running late. Memories of some past event can also trigger feelings of anger. It's these lingering images that we refuse to release that are the most harmful. We use a variety of ways to process our anger. We can be expressive, suppressive, or calming. When we get to a point where we can express our anger in a positive, constructive manner, we have reached a level of maturity that many strive for. We must be able to express our anger in such a way that we bring about resolution, while being respectful of ourselves and others.

In some situations, we tend to suppress our anger, especially if it's an old hurt, something that someone did to us in the past. We hold on to the same anger that we felt when it happened, and then we get mad all over again. How many times have we heard this or even felt this ourselves? Getting mad all over again does not bring closure to the wound. It's like that scab that miraculously appears to shield a wound in order to give it time to heal. If we leave it alone, the wound will heal. If we continually pick at it, we just keep opening up the old wound. That's how old anger is. We just keep picking at it until it becomes an open sore, one that never heals. This kind of suppressed anger can create a host of problems.

Aggressive Behavior — when you say to yourself: *I'm not going to get mad; I'm going to get even!* This type of thinking typically leads to a payback situation, and these never end respectfully.

Health problems — when you hold in your anger, it begins to affect you physically. High blood pressure usually occurs, and that can lead to a stroke.

Eating disorders, self-harm, and substance abuse are common among people who have suppressed anger issues.

People who are always cynical and hostile are often dealing with issues of suppressed anger. They typically find it difficult to talk about how they feel about past traumas, which has caused them to turn their anger inward. We cannot change what has happened in the past. We have to find a way to move past the hurt and past the anger.

One of the biggest obstacles to our personal growth is anger. When we fail to deal with our anger, it can destroy our ability to be happy. It is impossible to be happy if you are constantly in a state of anger. It also compromises any relationships that we might have. No one wants to be around a person who is always mad about something. It's how you look at life. If you get up in the morning angry about something that happened yesterday, trust me, you will find something to be angry about today. Life becomes a vicious cycle because of your angry state of mind; everything that happens just makes you angrier.

We have to learn to recognize when our anger becomes a problem and deal with it. When minor everyday situations, in which anger should not be an issue, send us off the deep end, we have to learn how to reduce our anger and manage it in a more positive, constructive way. If the intensity of our anger causes us to make bad decisions, often with adverse consequences, that's an indication that we are not controlling our anger. We are allowing our anger to control us. When our anger lasts too long and is unresolved, it just forms the basis for all subsequent anger to build on. We can be angry for so long that it becomes a way of life.

So, how do we let go of anger?

First, we have to determine who we're angry at. Often we are angry at someone else, when we need to be directing some of that anger at ourselves. When anger at someone else causes us to make a bad decision, we will quickly blame that person. But if we take a hard, truthful look at the cause of our anger, we may find that it leads right back to us. Until we get to the root of our anger, we cannot do what needs to be done to let it go.

What was your role in the situation? How could you have handled it differently? If you could change something in that situation, what would you change? I'm not saying that all situations that caused you to be angry were your fault. Certainly, people in our lives can intentionally or unintentionally do something to make us angry. We need to determine if our continued angry state is changing anything? It probably isn't. That person has probably gone on with their lives, not even realizing that you stopped at the point that they made you angry. Life goes on for them, and you have chosen to stay in the past. We all know of families that have stayed angry for generations. It gets to the point where they don't even remember what started it. Someone has to take a stand and say: *That's enough! I refuse to carry this anger any longer. I pray, Lord, that you help me release this demon spirit of anger that has taken control of my life.*

Second, we have to determine if we have learned anything from the past. We cannot expect different results if we keep doing the same thing. That's the definition of insanity. So, if your response to situations is always anger or negativity, then all of your future situations will probably be the same. Your mind is like a bank; it can only withdraw what has been deposited. So, if all of your thoughts are angry, all of your resulting actions will also be out of anger. If you have truly looked at the origin of your anger, there should be a lesson for you to learn. That's what life is—a lesson. And if we don't learn from our lessons, we will continue to repeat those lessons. How have you grown? How are you dealing with your present anger so that it doesn't become past anger that you are still dealing with tomorrow?

What can you do to resolve the anger that still lingers from the past? Do you even want to resolve it and get to a place of peace in your spirit? I'm convinced that some people don't want to change. Are you willing to do what needs to be done in order to bring about a peaceful resolution? When someone you love hurts you, it's very easy to become angry and confused. If we continue to dwell on these situations, grudges filled with resentment and hostility may take root. If we allow these negative feelings to crowd out our positive ones, we may find ourselves swallowed up in a sea of bitterness. We have to be prepared to make some changes in our lives. The way we've always handled things might not be in our best interest. We've got to be willing to take a long, hard look at the ugly things in our lives. It's easy to look at the good, but it takes a stronger effort to take a realistic look at some of our not-so-nice points.

Can you forgive others for the wrongs that they have done to you? Can you forgive yourself for some of the bad choices that you've made in the past? Forgiveness is the core of releasing past anger. Until we find the place of forgiveness, we will never get to the point of moving past the hurt, past the anger. Forgiveness cleanses your spirit. When we forgive, we move from the role of victim, and we release the control and power the offending person or situation has had on our life. It doesn't matter if the person who did you wrong apologizes or even acknowledges what they did to you. Forgiveness releases the hold that anger has on you. It frees you up for a more joyous existence. As you let go of grudges, you will no longer define yourself by your past hurts. I have forgiven people who have impacted my life greatly. I'm not going to tell you that it's been easy, but those people and situations no longer hold any power over me. Until you get to the point where you can release and let go of some of that anger, guess what the people who did you an injustice have over you? POWER!

Take control of your thoughts. Simply put, this means changing the way you think. When you find yourself thinking of past situations or circumstances that made you angry, don't dwell on them. If you continually think about things that make you angry, that adds fuel to that anger. We must learn to redirect our minds to the things that are good and pleasing to the Lord. Think of something funny instead. Look at a silly television program to make you laugh. That always works for me. I'm convinced that our God has a sense of humor. Since we are built in His image, He wants us to exist in a place of happiness and joy. How would you describe yourself? Happy? Bitter? Angry? What do you do when you think of something that made you mad? When was the last time you had a good laugh?

You want to associate yourself with people who are happy. The old saying, "misery loves company" is true, because the only people who want to associate with miserable, angry people are people who are also miserable and angry. You cannot improve your situation if you don't enlarge your territory; seek out new people and new adventures. If you are angry about something, find a true friend who will let you vent (that's another word for a pity party). They can let you know it's time to deal with it and get over it. If you feel someone has done a disservice to you, don't let it fester in your spirit. Recognize that it's not worth the effort, and let it go. If you can't, then pull that person aside and let them know how what they did or said affected you. When someone makes you angry, do you brush it off and move on, or do you tend to hold a grudge? How many times do you revisit old wounds?

Think of your past as a backpack that you've been carrying around all of your life. The older you are, the heavier your backpack becomes, particularly if you are carrying around old hurts and old anger. You may need to take an inventory of what you're carrying around. You may need to identify some past hurts that made you angry and put them in priority according to their level of importance. You may be carrying around baggage that is of no importance to your life today. Once you have done this, ask yourself if this is a memory worth holding onto? Are some of those memories weighing you down? Are they keeping you back from new experiences? Are they taking up space that you could fill with happy memories?

Recognize that this is a process. If you think about how long you have been holding onto some of your anger, you cannot expect to release it immediately. As with any process, you have to start. You cannot finish the race until you have taken the first step. Beating yourself up because you can't seem to get over something is not a method of self-improvement. Sometimes life beats us up to the point that we cannot get it back on track by ourselves. The word says, "We can do all things through Christ which strengthens us." But also understand that God has placed a calling on some people to help others. Don't be too afraid or prideful to seek help if you need it.

Sometimes people have a lot of anger inside of them as a result of things that have happened to them in the past—abuse, broken relationships, bereavement, etc. Maybe they feel that life has treated them badly. It's normal to have a lot of anger because of certain situations. Yes, sometimes life is unfair, and sometimes things don't work out the way we want them to or thought they would. However, holding on to past anger because of something that can't be changed will only damage your life now and in the future. That's how people become old and bitter.

You cannot change the past. We are only given one life, and we are not told when it's time for us to end this phase of our journey. It is very sad if you are living a life of anger and bitterness over something that you cannot change. Yesterday is gone, and we cannot get it back. We have to do all we can do to create a happy life now by releasing those past hurts and past anger. If you are angry about something that has happened in the past, you must realize that you don't have any control over that. It's past. You can take the control back in your life though. You can choose to stay angry at the world and allow it to destroy your happiness. Or, you can choose to let go of that anger, to heal, and to start living life to its fullest. God wants us to live life and live it more abundantly. We cannot live in the fullness of God if we are carrying ugly baggage from the past. Life is too short to waste. Shake it off and move on.

We all know what anger is. You may be angry over something that happened in the past that you had no control over. Anger is usually a normal, healthy emotion. But when you hold onto your anger, refusing to let it go, it can lead to health issues and possibly destructive behavior.

General

1. What is anger?

_____

_____

_____

_____

_____

2. How do you know if your anger is a problem?

_____

_____

_____

_____

_____

_____

3. What are some causes of your past anger?

_____

_____

_____

_____

_____

_____

4. What are some expressions of your anger—healthy and
    unhealthy?

_____

_____

_____

_____

_____

_____

Recognizing Your Anger

1. Who are you angry with?

_____

_____

_____

_____

_____

_____

2. How do you express your anger?

_____

_____

_____

_____

_____

_____

_____

3. Why are you angry?

_____

_____

_____

_____

_____

_____

_____

4. What problems does your unresolved anger cause?

_____

_____

_____

_____

_____

_____

_____

5. What is really pushing your buttons?

_____

_____

_____

_____

_____

_____

_____

6. Why?

_____

_____

_____

_____

_____

_____

Handling Your Anger

1. How can you control your anger?

_____

_____

_____

_____

_____

_____

_____

2. What are you willing to do to break the anger cycle in your life?

_____

_____

_____

_____

_____

_____

_____

3. What is the worst consequence of not dealing with your past anger?

_____

_____

_____

_____

_____

_____

4. What are some "dos" and "don'ts" of dealing with your anger?

_____

_____

_____

_____

_____

_____

5. What specific steps can you take to resolve your lingering anger issues?

_____

_____

_____

_____

_____

_____

Forgiveness

By Barry Maltese

If you look inside of your heart, you can find
forgiveness or at least the start.

And from that place where you can forgive, is where
Hope and Love also thrive and live.

And with each step that you try to take, and with that
chance that our heart might break,

Comes so much happiness and so much strength,
which alone can carry you a fantastic length.

For hate and anger will not get you there, and though
you say that you just don't care,

You can easily avoid the pain on which hate feeds…
the kind of pain that no one needs.

Just make the move, take the first stride, let go of the
thing known as "Foolish Pride."

Maybe then you can start to repair the past

Into something strong, that will mend and last.

Learning How to Forgive

Forgivingness is so important to your overall well being. It is about cleansing your spirit, and being released from the past. Forgiveness is a process that doesn't happen overnight. It takes some time to be able to forgive the other person, and then we have to work on forgiving ourselves. I beat myself up for a long time after I stopped blaming someone else for the shape I was in. I realized that some of the decisions I had made were not the wisest decisions, and I was stuck living with the consequences of those decisions. So, when I stopped blaming someone else, I took a look at myself and began to think I was the stupid one. How could I have been so stupid? How could I have let myself get in to this position?

We make some bad decisions, and we learn from them. I called my abuser several years ago, and I apologized to him for all of the things that I did in our relationship that I should not have done, and all of those things that I should have done that I didn't. His response was that I didn't have to do that for him. But it wasn't for him. It was for my healing, my growth, and my development.

To be able to be all that you can be, you've got to forgive. But you have to work toward this. You will not automatically get to a point where you can forgive someone who has done something to hurt you in your past. A little at a time, it makes you feel stronger.

I have learned how to forgive, but I have not forgotten. Forgiveness is a choice. You don't have to forgive, but by not forgiving, you hold in all of that. When you refuse to forgive, you hold onto the anger, bitterness, sense of betrayal, or whatever it was that hurt you. That person still has control over you, because as long as you are unwilling to forgive, they still have the ability to push those same buttons that they pushed before that got you angry. So we have to understand that forgiveness is a process that does not happen overnight. It's a process that takes small steps to yield big results.

We also have to understand who it is we have to forgive. Most of the time, we do not concentrate on everyone in our lives who has done us wrong. While we're looking at everyone else, we have to get to the point where we can look at ourselves. A lot of where we are is a direct result of choices we made. And the consequences of those choices are what land us in the situations we find ourselves in. The first time my abuser hit me was his fault, but the second and subsequent times were my fault, because I didn't leave after the first time. So the abuse I endured was partially the result of choices I made.

I am in no way saying that the abuse that is suffered is the victim's fault. Taking on the responsibility of someone else's actions will only delay our ability to forgive ourselves. I had to get to the point where I not only had to forgive him, but I had to forgive myself. We all eventually get to the point where we say to ourselves: *How could I have been so stupid? How could I have allowed myself to get into this situation – again?* We have to learn that forgiveness is not just about other people, but we must also forgive ourselves for some of the choices that we made in the past.

Forgiveness does not mean that you will reconcile with someone who has mistreated you. It doesn't mean that at all. I've gotten to a point where I have forgiven my abuser and myself. Because of that, he no longer controls me. Another misconception is that forgiveness depends upon whether or not the person who mistreated you apologizes. Forgiveness doesn't have anything to do with whether or not the person even acknowledges or admits that they did something wrong to you. Forgiveness has nothing to do with that. If another person's behavior was the primary factor in forgiveness for our healing, then we would never be healed. We cannot control another person's behavior.

I had a discussion with a client who had been abused. This is the story she told:

> My first child's father had been sent to prison, and there was another man with whom I had decided to be just friends. I let this man know that I loved the man in prison, but that if he wanted to, we could be just friends.

> It went on like this for a year and a half, and then I got pregnant. In his mind, my pregnancy was an indication that our relationship was more than a friendship. But it wasn't in my mind. After two kids and numerous beatings, I had to realize that in the beginning, I had made the decision to deal with this man, but I also had to realize that an affair of the heart was a tricky thing. I had to forgive myself for leading that man on in the beginning. In his mind, it must be love, because I had sex with him and had his baby.

> I talked to him and told him that we could just be good parents and raise our children, but that I still loved the father of my oldest child. That's when the abuse really started. He couldn't understand.

> For a long time, he and my brothers would fight because of the abuse. The last time he beat me was for two days straight. He dragged me out of my house and took me to a motel. He broke my tooth, beat me, and stomped on me. The Lord took care of my kids and sent my brothers to look after them.

> As he beat me, I just continued to talk to the Lord and said to Him, "If it's my time to go, just make sure someone looks after my kids."

> I continued to pray, and I never responded to his beating me. After every hit with the bat, every kick, I just kept talking to the Lord.

> "If I'm supposed to die, I know you have got something

good prepared for my kids down here and for me up there."

But I didn't die. I'm not sure what made him stop. It must have been the Lord, because I thought he was going to kill me that night. I had to realize that I had led this man on in the beginning, and in being so childish, that we created a child together. I didn't realize this man was in love with me like he was, and I disrespected him and his feelings. That still didn't give him the right to do what he did to me, but I accepted that I was wrong, also, for playing with this man's feelings. I have forgiven myself, and I apologized to him. He didn't have to apologize to me. I knew he would never admit that all of this was a result of the fact that he loved me and I didn't love him in return. He would never admit that he did anything wrong. In his mind, everything that had happened to me, I had brought on myself.

That's what an unforgiving spirit does. You never get over the anger, and that anger will overtake you whenever you see that person. We go through life hanging onto this anger, and it begins to fester like a sore. Every time we see that person, we pick at our anger and pick at it again and again. We make it so bad that it becomes like gangrene — mental gangrene. The only solution is to cut it off. Eventually this mental gangrene will start to have physical effects on your body. It can cause high blood pressure, substance abuse, etc.

We have to understand that a spirit of forgiveness is about ourselves. When you can get to the point where you recognize your role in the situation, you are well on your way towards forgiveness. We have to accept our responsibility, whatever role that was. We have to take a good, long look at it. We need to get to the point where we can say to ourselves: *I made some bad choices, and I messed up. Now, I forgive myself for the mistakes that I've made, but I'm going to learn from that, not make that mistake again, and go on with my life.* That's what forgiveness is.

Until we learn how to forgive, we cannot move on to even hope to have any type of a meaningful relationship with anyone else. This is because we have not gotten to the point where we are in a good relationship with ourselves. If I asked you to list everyone you have a relationship with, would you remember yourself? Probably not! You have to have a relationship with yourself. That means you have to accept all of yourself – the good, the bad, and the ugly.

We have to learn how to forgive ourselves for bad choices we make. Often that is difficult, because the decisions we make not only affect us, but most of the time, also affect our children. We become angry at ourselves when we see that happen, and we forget that we are allowed to make bad decisions. Everyone is allowed to do that. What we don't want to do is to keep harping on those bad decisions so that they affect how we think, because that puts us in a position where we keep making bad decisions.

If you are angry about something today, and you make a decision based on that anger, the consequences of that decision are going to affect you tomorrow. We have to learn how to get past that so that the hurt begins to heal. We have to know that whatever happened then was then. We cannot go back and change the past, but we can think about where we are today and where we want to be tomorrow. We must recognize that forgiveness helps us, and by not forgiving, we keep ourselves in a struggle. We're struggling with our spirit, our minds, and everyone else. We constantly struggle with relationships, trying to get past the past. That's what happens when we have allowed ourselves to be put in a situation where someone has done us wrong.

Client: I'm still dealing with trying to forgive my father for not being there for me when I was growing up.

Coach: So if I'm hearing you correctly, the reason you don't deal with your father now is because of something that he did to you when you were a child? You haven't let go of that anger.

86

You are still holding onto that anger because he left you when you were four.

Client: He knew that my mom had died and my grandmother was struggling, and he lived around the corner.

Coach: You can have a spirit of forgiveness for your dad, but you don't have to forget. That just means you have released all that anger for what he didn't do. Forgiveness is a process. You don't forget what has happened, but if you can think about what they did or didn't do and you don't get angry, that's when your spirit is calling out for you to forgive and move on.

Client: You are right. When I'm around my dad, I don't want to hear him say anything about when my sisters were little, because I didn't have those experiences with him. I have to work on that. How do I do that?

Coach: Pray and ask the Lord to bring peace to your spirit in your relationship with your father. What you want is not a relationship with your father, but peace in your spirit. Ask the Lord to give you that sense of peace. One day, you will see him and not get angry, and then you'll be ready to have a conversation with him.

Client: When I hurt him, I feel like I'm getting even with him. I will ask the Lord to help me with my relationship with my father.

Coach: The act of forgiveness is like a mental bath; it's cleansing something that can poison us from within. Let it go to release that poison. It is not easy, but it is a process.

Forgiveness is the single most important thing that brings peace to your soul and to your spirit. And, it provides harmony in your life. You have to get to the point where you have the peace to pass on to your children, regardless of what they have witnessed. People talk about generational curses. Well anger, hatred, and bitterness—those are generational curses. What we do as women is that we hate or are angry at our children's father, and we have a tendency to pass that spirit of hatred on to our children. We are raising a generation of angry children, and we have no idea why they're angry. We must look at the dominant spirit that flows through our homes. Is it a spirit of love, peace, and joy or a spirit of anger, bitterness, and hatred? Have you been so angry with your abuser that the poison within you is starting to affect your children? Are the consequences of a decision you made not only affecting you, but are they affecting your children's health?

Forgiveness provides us with a sense of harmony in our lives so that we can get rid of all those toxic negative feelings. These have a tendency to take root in our spirit, and we become that negative, bitter, angry person. So many of our senior citizens are angry, because they look back over their lives at some of the choices that they made, and that spirit of anger—that unforgiving spirit—begins to take root. We all know people who haven't talked to their kinfolk in years—so long that they don't even remember why they are not talking. That's what an unforgiving spirit does. It can rob you of some of the joys of life. We have to give ourselves the gift of forgiveness so that we can allow our spirit to flow and live life to its fullest.

Benefits of forgiveness include healthier relationships, greater spiritual well-being, and less stress. Forgiveness can relieve hostility and lowers your risk of substance abuse. Not forgiving repeats the cycle of anger and bitterness. Forgiveness is a choice. The first step is to decide if we want to forgive.

How do we get to the point of forgiveness?

Realize that whatever you feel towards the person who hurt you does not affect that person in the slightest. In all likelihood, they have gone on with life and probably don't even remember.

Understand that the best revenge against your enemies is to live a successful and happy life. Want to get even with someone who tried to destroy you? Show them and show yourself (and the world) that the obstacles they tried to create were not significant enough to disable you and/or destroy you.

The second best revenge is to turn that intention of harm into something good. It requires a strong spirit to find the proverbial silver lining in the dark cloud. You should think of your enemy as a stepping stone. Your haters should become people who have helped you to grow. You cannot live in this life and not have unfortunate things happen to you. What you can do is to see those situations as tests that will either destroy or strengthen you. If you've been *through* something, it didn't destroy you. Take what you learned, and become a better person because of it. There is joy on the other side of through!

What are the good things that resulted from this painful experience? Sometimes you can focus for so long on the negative aspects of this experience that you can't even see anything good. As hard as it may be, take a look at the problem from a completely new angle; look at the positive side. The first item on that list is that you survived it. What else that was positive came out of it? See if you can identify ten positive outcomes of this experience.

Who helped you? In every tragic situation that happens, there are usually unsung heroes. Those are the people who helped out. In your own hellish experience, remember the people who helped you. Think about what they did to help you get through—their kindness and unselfishness. Find someone to help you through your ordeal. Begin to practice what you have learned from your helper.

Perhaps you need to look at the bigger picture. There are times when the trials and tribulations that you go through in life are not even about you. Was your experience to give something to someone else? Of course, we would all prefer not to go through hardships—for the Lord to bless someone else—but this happens. The blessing is also in the giving and not just the receiving. Someone may have been blessed by the help they gave you. Perhaps your trial provided an opportunity for others to rise to an occasion to provide you with help and support.

Be patient with yourself. If you've stewed over this problem for a long time, charting a new direction is going to take some time. As you try to get past this old hurt, you'll make mistakes. Forgive and be kind to yourself. Just as extreme physical pain takes time to heal, extreme emotional pain has a profound effect on the body as well. Give yourself time to heal — physically and emotionally. Eat well, rest, and give yourself permission to feel the emotions and process them. Don't bottle up the pain.

Learn that by forgiving, you untie the last shred of control that the person has over you. The best way to free yourself from the person trying to do you harm — and everything negative that is associated with them — is to forgive. Once you untie the bindings and loosen yourself from that person's hold, you can start walking away from them and away from the pain. Forgiveness is a selfish act; it is for you and not the other party. It is a cleansing of your spirit. Freeing yourself through forgiveness is like freeing yourself from the chains of bondage or freeing yourself from prison.

You've got to balance trust with wisdom. You can be assured that not everyone in your life is trustworthy, but everyone is also not out to get you. Let your painful memories protect you from future hurts, but don't allow those memories to block your future blessings. As author, Rose Sweet, writes, "A lack of trust is sometimes simply recognizing another's limitations."

Forgiveness does not mean acceptance of wrong behavior. It does require you to acknowledge it. If you must continue to interact with someone who has wronged you, who continually offers an apology, only to follow it up with more bad behavior, you don't have to nor should you trust such a person. This person isn't likely to ever be trustworthy. You must keep this person at "an arm's length." You know the old saying, "Feed them out of a long-handled spoon!" While it does not benefit you to torment yourself over this person's actions, you should not be their willing victim. Acknowledge, and then move on.

A person who wants to reconcile with you must do their part: offer a sincere apology, promise not to repeat the offense (or similar ones), make amends, and give it time. This is the definition of repentance. If you don't see any sincerity, understand that forgiving that person is a benefit to you, not to the offender.

You need to use wisdom to avoid repeating the hurt. This will probably require you to avoid those individuals who have harmed you in the first place. It would be wise to balance forgiveness against the certain knowledge that evil exists, and some people enjoy harming others.

Stop dwelling on the hurt. How many times do you find yourself telling the story about how badly you were hurt and how horribly you were wronged? How many times a day do you think about this hurt? It is a stake driven into your heart that keeps you from moving away from this hurt. Instead, concentrate on the lessons that you've learned, and move on. It's the kindest thing you can do for yourself, your friends, and your family. Negativity is depressing—physically, mentally, spiritually, and emotionally.

Retrain your thinking. If you understand the Law of Attraction, you'll realize that any negative thoughts will only bring about negative energy. If your enemy comes to mind, just wish the best for them. This will neutralize the hatred that will eventually take over your heart, and soon the good that you wish for another will rebound back to you. When you are able to return a blessing for hatred, you are well on the path to wholeness. It may seem empty and even hypocritical at first, but keep trying. All habits, whether good or bad, take a repetitive action to become a part of the new you. After a while, the anger and pain that has burned in your heart for so long will disappear, and you'll experience a peace unlike anything you have felt. This technique forces your mind to change your belief about life. You will begin to say to yourself: *It's time to let it go and move on.*

Don't lose your perspective on life. The hurtful actions of your enemy are, no doubt, hurtful to you, but the rest of the world goes on. The only person suffering is you. Validate the meaning of your life not by the negative experiences, but by those positive things in your life. Don't lose sight of the fact that the other people in your life are not involved and do not deserve to be treated badly.

Forgiveness is a cleansing of your spirit. It allows you to have a better future — one that is based on the assurance that your past hurts will not be the final word. When you give up your negative thoughts about the situation, it ushers in the possibility of a better future. You cannot have healthy relationships without forgiveness. If you continue to hold onto things that happened in the past, you cannot have a loving relationship with anyone, including yourself. It doesn't matter what the situation was; it is only by making peace with that person who you think may have "done you wrong" that you can improve your chances of a healthy relationship. Forgiveness releases you from that self-imposed prison of the past to a liberated person who is at peace with their memories. Do not be mistaken; forgiveness is not forgetfulness, but it does involve accepting the promise that the future can be more than dwelling on memories of past hurts.

There is no future in the past. You cannot see where you are going if you are constantly looking behind you. Your past is past. You have got to put down that old baggage if you want to create a new and exciting future for yourself. You are never too old to start over. Begin again! Starting today, make a decision to let go of past hurts, confusion, and resentments. Old wounds are like an old song that you hear on the radio. All memories, whether good or bad, have a drawing power and pull your attention to them over and over. They can take energy and hope from us, preventing us from starting again, or inspiring us to keep going.

When you forgive, you let go, and you restore yourself to basic goodness and health. When you forgive you give up resentment, revenge, and obsession so that your faith can be restored, not only in yourself, but in life itself. Your unwillingness to do this only causes you harm. Forgiveness is not something you have to do, but something you must allow to flow through you. It is not a word or a gesture but an emotion that happens when we step away from the consciousness of our human nature and allow God's grace to express through us, to forgive through us. You'll know when you are there, because you can feel the radiant and warm rays of the flow of divine love dissolving all hurt, all bitterness, all sense of injustice. You become aware that you are free and no longer a captive of the power of another person.

Forgiveness helps you move forward. The benefits from forgiveness are for you, not anyone else. It cleanses your system of the poison that will surely fester and cause illness and continued misery if not released.

Give yourself the gift of forgiveness.

Forgiveness is a gift that you give to yourself. It's not for the betterment of anyone other than you. It doesn't matter if the person who offended you apologizes or even recognizes that they hurt you. Ultimately, forgiveness is a cleansing of your spirit so that you can move on with your life. Forgiveness dares you to imagine a future that is not predicated on a past hurt. It challenges you to give up those destructive thoughts that block your blessings.

The Desire to Forgive

1. What does forgiveness mean to you?

_____

_____

_____

_____

_____

_____

2. What are the benefits to you of forgiving someone?

_____

_____

_____

_____

_____

_____

3. Why is it so easy for you to hold a grudge?

_____

_____

_____

_____

_____

_____

_____

4. Who are you holding a grudge against? Why?

_____

_____

_____

_____

_____

_____

_____

Steps to Forgiveness

1. What can you do to reach a state of forgiveness?

_____

_____

_____

_____

_____

_____

2. What good things came as a result of the hurt? Make a list:

_____

_____

_____

_____

_____

_____

3. What did you learn from the experience to help you grow?

_____

_____

_____

_____

_____

_____

_____

4. How can forgiveness add value to your life?

_____

_____

_____

_____

_____

_____

_____

5. What can you do to retrain your thinking about this person?

_____

_____

_____

_____

_____

_____

An Unforgiving Spirit

1. What are some of the effects of holding onto a grudge?

_____

_____

_____

_____

_____

_____

2. How does an unforgiving spirit affect your life?

_____

_____

_____

_____

_____

_____

_____

3. How does it affect the lives of people around you?

_____

_____

_____

_____

_____

_____

_____

4. How does an unforgiving spirit impact your relationships with people?

_____

_____

_____

_____

_____

_____

Forgiving Yourself

1. What have you done that makes you feel shame or guilt?

_____

_____

_____

_____

_____

_____

2. How can you overcome your sense of guilt?

_____

_____

_____

_____

_____

_____

_____

3. What can you do to retrain your thinking about yourself?

_____

_____

_____

_____

_____

_____

_____

4. What can you do to learn to love yourself again?

_____

_____

_____

_____

_____

_____

_____

Your Stepping Stone

Author Unknown

Over the years, when you've suffered a setback
and the reason for it seemed unknown,
Did you ever consider that it was a lesson,
and that failure's a stepping stone?

How you respond and what you learn from it
shows the world how much you have grown.
You'll climb a bit higher toward the peak of success,
making failure a stepping stone.

For *you* make the choice in the way that you see it.
It is *your* decision alone.
You can stall in self-pity or keep moving upward,
making failure a stepping stone.

So join all the people who've ever succeeded,
and practice the courage they've shown.
Learn from your losses, but keep climbing higher,
and make failure your stepping stone.

Life After Failure

Everybody fails at something at some point in their lives. It may be a failing grade at school, a failure to get that promotion on your job, or you may fail at love. Success and failure are two sides of the same coin. Although you wish to experience only successes and no failures, you can't have one without the other. Failure, like success, is a fact of life. It is always lurking just around the corner, and you have no choice but to learn to deal with failure if you are to be successful.

How do you define failure? Who do you consider a failure? Is there something you didn't do well, or perhaps your dream went south with all of your hopes? Failure is not necessarily a lack of success, but rather the inability to do what you can do, the best way you can. Thinking of yourself as a failure can become an unintentional habit—those times that you count small setbacks as an identifier of failure. Sometimes you define yourself as a failure when you simply indulge yourself in laziness.

Do you fail sometimes? Yes, but your failure is simply a lack of the necessary insight to do the best you can do. A major part of getting past your past is acceptance. When you finally learn to accept that failure is a part of life, you can begin to take the next step in your journey called life. Life is full of unexpected events, some good and some bad. You have to learn how to build on the positives and learn from the negatives.

Many people think failure is an unwanted end of something that they tried to do, when in actuality, it's just the beginning. At some point in all of our lives, we have failed at something, and it would be easy to think of ourselves a failures. Great achievers don't give up; they keep on trying. They hold onto a self-belief and don't allow their failures to become their focal point. It is impossible for you to move forward if you believe you are a failure. You have to be able to separate life's unfortunate events from your self-worth and your future actions. Successful people are not immune to failure. It is how they process it and what they do about the failure that makes a difference.

What separates people who enjoy success from the majority who end up never getting what they want is how they respond to failure. It is not that successful people don't fail or haven't failed at something. It is what you do about failure that makes a big difference.

There are three common ways that you can respond to failure.

Do you make excuses, lay blame, and give up? Are you one of those people who constantly whine when they don't get their way? Do you come up with a hundred different excuses as to why something didn't work out like you thought it would? Do you always find someone else to blame your misfortune on?

How many times have you said to yourself something like…?

It's not fair.

I'm too young.

I'm too old.

If you are in this group, you will ultimately feel frustrated at your repeated attempts and subsequent failures, and you will eventually give up. You will settle into mediocrity and resign yourself to the belief that everything you want is out of your reach.

Do you keep trying the same thing over and over again? If so, you have a lot more determination than if you were in the first group, but the outcome is generally the same. When you don't get the desired outcome, you won't quit, you'll jump right back into action. Do you think your failure was a result of not trying hard enough?

Do you think to yourself…?

If I just keep on trying and try a little harder, surely I will eventually succeed.

No matter how many times you fail, you will just keep trying harder and harder. If you are in this group, it is possible for you to accomplish some of your goals. If you set small, incremental goals, with enough time and effort, you may eventually succeed. If, on the other hand, you set exceptional goals, like opening your own business, you will not be successful by simply trying over and over again. If you keep using the same approach, you will keep getting the same results. People in this group can be so dogged in their pursuit that they fail to see that the actions they think will produce the desired results are actually sabotaging their efforts.

Do you get feedback, change your strategy, and take action until you succeed? If you are in this category, you have a different perception of failure. You see it as an opportunity to grow. You tend to look into the failure and derive feedback so that you can change your strategy the next time. If the initial strategy was insufficient, or you didn't take enough action, you will use this feedback to change your tactics and try again. If you still don't succeed, repeat the analysis, get feedback, and take another approach until you get what you want. Of course, if you are in this group, you tend to be more realistic so as to minimize permanent failure. This group views failure as life trying to teach them a lesson. As I stated in another chapter, life is about lessons. Until you learn them, you will continually make the same mistake. So remember that every time you don't get what you want, it is life giving you feedback. It is this continuous feedback that you need to help adjust your approach until you reach your goal.

Getting your life back on track after a failure is not always an easy task. You have to look at life differently in order to motivate yourself back into action.

How do you look at things differently?

You have to know your limits. What are your strengths and weaknesses? If you want to reduce your chances of making the same mistakes as before, you have to know what you can and cannot do. You want to set goals that will challenge you to reach for higher heights, but you don't want to stress yourself out. Challenging yourself can sometimes help to identify your limitations. There is always room for improvement. You were born with a gift, and it's a part of your journey to discover what that is.

Stop comparing yourself. It's natural to compare yourself with someone you think either has it "more together," or that you feel is in worse shape than you are. What we don't know is what their "story" is. Do you want to experience what they did in order to be in the position they're in? Sometimes you can concentrate on other people's success and not even realize that it only torments your spirit to the point that you can lose your passion and confidence in the things that you are good at. We are created equal, but you have your own strengths and abilities. We are instructed in **Galatians 6:4**: *"Let each one prove what his own work is, and then he will have cause for exultation in regard to himself alone, and not in comparison with the other person."*

Don't let the expectations of others define your success. The expectations of our immediate family members, friends, teachers, coworkers, and others should only be considered if they coincide with your own expectations. Sometimes it becomes a hindrance to your growth as a person to base your capabilities on someone else's definition. As a result, you end up trying to please people. People pleasers never find true success and are usually unable to bounce back from failure. Learn to be yourself, and let your true colors shine through.

Be realistic. You have to be woman enough to face your biggest mistakes and their consequences. It takes a stronger person to admit that they didn't do something right and move on than to blame themself forever for being a total failure. Look at the situation, and try to sort things out. What did you do right, and what went wrong? Doing better the next time and not making the same mistakes is as simple as that. Remember that your failures and mistakes don't define you, and they surely don't make you a lesser person.

Stop taking yourself so seriously. You have to find the humor in life — from the simple things, all the way up to the complex — despite all of the chaos. You should live your life so you have something to laugh about every day. Does it bother you when people laugh at you? Of course it does; it bothers everyone. If what you did is funny, laugh with them. It's better to have someone to laugh with than to go through life with no laughter at all.

Share yourself. You would be amazed at how brightening up a person's day by sharing positive thoughts can actually brighten your life. You really do reap what you sow. Give a little love, and it all comes back to you. Don't just sit there pondering life's failures; sometimes you have to be the one to get involved, and explore all the possibilities that life has to offer. Be a blessing to others. Just go and have a life!

Seize the day. We have to learn how to live each day as if it is our last, and to count our blessings every day — literally. It is the only way we can appreciate how marvelous the gift of life is.

But failure is painful, right? Successful people would disagree. To them, failure is a part of winning, and their sense of value is not dependent on the wins or the failures. You have to develop beliefs that will allow you to take advantage of negatives and turn them into your advantages.

I found an article that has ten rules to live by to turn you failure into success:

1. Failure renews my humility, sharpens my objectivity, and makes me more resilient.

2. I take the challenge seriously but I do not take myself too seriously.

3. The more I fail, the more I succeed, and then failure is a part of the process of achieving my objectives.

4. Failure is temporary when I use it as an opportunity to try new ideas.

5. I learn more from failure than from success.

6. Negative feedback is information that helps me correct my course so that I stay on target.

7. I am paid for the number of times I fail.

8. My self-esteem is not based on the reactions of others, but on my own sense of virtue.

9. The unkindness of others reminds me that I need to be kind to myself.

10. It takes courage to fail, because nobody ever got ahead without taking risks.

"There are always challenges at every stage in our lives. Overcoming them is what life is all about."

What separates successful people from those who never seem to get what they want is how they respond to failure. Failure is a natural part of life. It is crazy to think that you will succeed at everything you do. It's what you do with those failures that ultimately make the difference in your life.

Pattern One: Give Up

1. What are some excuses you can use to account for your failure(s)?

_____

_____

_____

_____

_____

_____

2. Who do you blame your failure on? Why?

_____

_____

_____

_____

_____

_____

3. What typically happens to your dream if you are a
Pattern One?

_____

_____

_____

_____

_____

_____

_____

4. What can you do to overcome this?

_____

_____

_____

_____

_____

_____

_____

Pattern Two: Over and Over

1. What are the characteristics if you are in this group?

_____

_____

_____

_____

_____

2. What did you do to meet your goals?

_____

_____

_____

_____

_____

_____

3. What is your future strategy to meet your goals?

_____

_____

_____

_____

_____

_____

4. How are you sabotaging your own efforts for success?

_____

_____

_____

_____

_____

_____

5. How will your future strategy change your outcome?

_____

_____

_____

_____

_____

_____

Pattern Three: Strategy Change

1. If you are in this group, how do you look at your failure?

_____

_____

_____

_____

_____

_____

_____

2. Why didn't you get the results you anticipated?

_____

_____

_____

_____

_____

_____

3. What actions are you going to take?

_____

_____

_____

_____

_____

_____

_____

4. How are you going to change your strategy?

_____

_____

_____

_____

_____

_____

_____

5. How committed are you to your success?

_____

_____

_____

_____

_____

_____

_____

General

1. What is your definition of failure?

_____

_____

_____

_____

_____

_____

2. What is your definition of a successful person?

_____

_____

_____

_____

_____

_____

_____

3. How do successful people deal with failure?

_____

_____

_____

_____

_____

_____

_____

4. How do you deal with failure?

_____

_____

_____

_____

_____

_____

_____

5. What are some ways to get past failures?

_____

_____

_____

_____

_____

_____

As You Travel Through Life...

Author Unknown

As you travel through life,
there are always those times
When decisions just have to be made —
When the choices are hard,
and solutions seem scarce,
And the rain seems to soak your parade.

There are some situations where all you can do
Is simply let go and move on;
Gather your courage and choose a direction
That carries you toward a new dawn.

So pack up your troubles, and take a step forward.
The process of change can be tough,
But think about all the excitement ahead
If you can be stalwart enough!

There might be adventures you never imagined
Just waiting around the next bend,
And wishes and dreams just about to come true
In ways you can't yet comprehend!

Perhaps you'll find friendships
that spring from new things
As you challenge your status quo,
And learn there are so many options in life,
and so many ways you can grow.

Perhaps you'll go places you never expected
And see things that you've never seen,
Or travel to fabulous, faraway worlds
And wonderful spots in between!

Perhaps you'll find warmth and affection and caring
And somebody special who's there
To help you stay centered and listen with interest
To stories and feelings you share.

Perhaps you'll find comfort
in knowing your friends
Are supportive of all that you do
And believe that whatever decisions you make,
They'll be the right choices for you.

So keep putting one foot in front of the other
And taking your life day by day.
There's a brighter tomorrow
that's just down the road.
Don't look back! You're not going that way!

Getting Past Your Past

We all have regrets—things in our past that we just hold on to. How often have you said or done things that you wished you hadn't, or regretted dreams or goals that you put on hold that went unfulfilled? Someone might have done something to you, or they did not do something for you—or maybe you had unexpected circumstances that took your life off the course that you thought you were on. Sometimes we end up in situations that we didn't plan on. Things happen, over the course of our lives, that changes our situations.

Do you have regrets over some past mistakes and decisions that you made? One of the reasons why I think you continue to think about your past regrets is that you didn't plan on making mistakes. I guarantee you that nobody sets out to make mistakes, but that is a part of life. You go through life, and sometimes you make bad choices, and then you beat yourself up for the choices that you made. I beat myself up for a long time, because it was my decision to stay in an abusive marriage. Consequently, I lost my home, my car, and my job. I lost a lot of stuff. At the time, I thought I had lost everything, but as long as you are able to say that, you have not lost everything. You still have life and one more chance.

A new dawn brings a new beginning. You make bad choices and then assume things are going to turn out differently. When they don't, you have regrets about those decisions. Most of the time, you are able to put most of your regrets behind you. On a daily basis, you may say to yourself: *Shucks, I should have done that or I should not have done that.* Those kinds of regrets you can put behind you. When you have big regrets from your past, sometimes it's hard for you to get past those. You get stuck on the "could've, would've, should've" syndrome. That's when your mind repeatedly returns to the thought that if you had only done this or that, then things would have turned out differently. That thought keeps playing over and over in your mind, and instead of helping you to get rid of those regrets, it just adds fuel to the fire. What you want to do is to figure out a way to get past those thoughts so that you can move on.

Where you are today is a direct result of choices you made yesterday. So you have to understand that where you'll be tomorrow will be due to the decisions that you make today. Consequently, you don't want to make decisions today based on some past regrets, because you may not be making the best decisions. You'll want to learn how to get past that. One way to do that is to concentrate on what is today. Yesterday is gone, and you cannot change what has already happened. Whether it was a good day or a bad day, whether you made good decisions or bad ones, it's gone — so don't concentrate on that. You've got to start concentrating on what's happening today and what can be tomorrow in your future. It's impossible to focus on what's happening right now and where you want to go tomorrow while you're concentrating on yesterday. You have to make a decision: Are you going to constantly think about what you did wrong, or are you going to focus on where you are today? Even if this is not where you thought you were going to be, this is where you are. How do you move on from today to make tomorrow better?

A lot of people grow old with regrets. We all know people who are old and bitter. These are people who are living their lives in yesterday. They regret some of the things that they did, or shouldn't have done, and regret some of the things that they never accomplished in their lives. You can easily get to the point where you regret yesterday and stop living for today. The first thing you've got to do is to accept that this is how it is right now. It may not be how you want it, but that's the way it is. If all of us could have dealt our own deck of life cards, probably none of us would have dealt the hand we got. I would have been born into wealth and married into wealth. All of us would have chosen a different path. But you've got to accept that this is where you are right now. It doesn't mean that this is where you have to be forever, but this is your starting point.

Whatever got you here doesn't matter. The fact is, this is where you are. You must always remember that wherever you are, no matter how bad you think it is, there is someone worse off than you. When you have reached the phase in your life where you are living with past regrets and have moved on, remember that this is just part of your journey called life. On your tombstone will be a date of birth, a dash, and a date of death. The only thing that matters is what's in between—the dash—because the day you were born is only important to you, and the day you die is important to your loved ones, for a while. The only thing that matters is the dash. Everyday can be important. Every day can be an accomplishment. Accept where you are, and build upon it to make a better tomorrow. Start now by letting go of some small things that you regret.

Forgiveness is a part of letting go of the past. It's acknowledging the role that you played in your situation. It's accepting that a certain amount of the situation you're in is your fault. The first time my abuser hit me was his fault, but the second time he hit me was my fault, because I chose to stay. You have to get to the point where you can acknowledge the role you played in your situation. What part of it was your fault? What part did someone else play? You have to work on forgiveness. Forgiveness releases the hold that person has on your life. They no longer control your emotions and how you will respond. Those same buttons they pushed to get you to respond a certain way won't work anymore. It releases you from all of that past hurt and anger, and it releases you from seeking revenge on those people whom you trusted, who have hurt you somewhere in your past.

It's a process to be able to handle the past hurts and move on to today's lessons. You've got to stop blaming someone else to be able to learn lessons from the past. Life is full of lessons, and until we learn from them—trust me—those lessons just keep on repeating themselves. The path to get from where you are to where you want to be is all about learning life's lessons. We all know women who appear to be the nicest of women but always end up with men that treat them badly. Do you wonder why she keeps getting these men who are wrong for her? It's because she hasn't learned her lesson. How many times have you said to yourself: *What was I thinking? I knew better. I can't believe I'm in this same situation — again!* So you have a short pity party; just don't let your party last a lifetime! A woman once told me that she has a good time at her pity parties, and we laughed about it. When you think of it, the pity parties can make you feel better. The problem is that you can't stay at that party for very long. Have your tantrum, pick yourself up, and move on. Don't hold onto your regrets. Learn the lesson. Learn from your past.

Here are some things that you can do to help you along your journey:

Think about what you're going to say before you speak. Once you say something, you can't take it back. It's out in the Universe. If your words cause hurt or damage to someone's character, it may not be repairable. Regrets from your words and the subsequent healing can take a long time. This is a spiritual journey. It comes with spiritual maturity. Ask the Lord to help you to think before you speak. Accept the reality that you don't have any control over anyone except yourself, and you have to control what comes out of your mouth.

Life is about learning that everyone doesn't go by your script. Keep your drama in your own movie. You can't control how anyone else reacts or responds, or what they're going to do. Disappointment happens when you expect another person to live out your drama. When they don't, you may become disappointed. You wonder why they just couldn't do it your way; it would have been so much simpler — for you.

It's important for you to remember the lessons you have

learned, and it is just as important for you to let go of the ones that you can't learn anything from. Let it go! Sometimes, things happen in our lives, and we cannot understand why. Bad things do happen to good people, and sometimes it is not up to us to understand why. My beloved Pastor died suddenly the day that I was over at his home. I was totally devastated and asked God why He took him from us. Surely, at his age, he had not finished all that God wanted him to do. There are some things that are not meant for us to understand. God's ways are not our ways. Sometimes you are not going to understand, so don't beat yourself up asking why something happened.

Concentrating on your past, and on past regrets, impedes your ability to move forward. If you don't move and keep up, life will pass you by. The world doesn't stop because you are living in the past, dwelling on past mistakes and bad decisions, trying to figure out what happened yesterday. Every day gives you a new opportunity. A NEW DAWN BRINGS A NEW BEGINNING. Every day when the sun comes up, you have another opportunity to start all over again. So whatever you did yesterday, leave it there. He's giving you a brand new slate.

Sometimes painful experiences will occur, and it can really stifle your ability to be able to move on and make progress. You must understand that you sabotage yourself by carrying baggage. Everybody has baggage that they bring to the table. It's like a backpack filled with stuff or a trunk full of stuff that you just continue to pile more things on top of. You don't even know what's at the bottom of the pile, but you keep carrying it with you into the future. It's like the junk drawer you have in your home. You're not sure what's in it, but you don't want to throw it away, just in case you might need it again. One thing is for certain: If you ramble around in that junk drawer long enough, you're going to prick your finger on something. You are going to get hurt. That's the same way it is with rambling around in yesterday's regrets. At some point, you're going to dredge up something that's going to hurt. You need to learn how to sift through the baggage. What baggage do you need to bring with you, and what baggage do you need to leave in yesterday?

You have to learn how to clean out that mental junk drawer, or just close it and not open it again. Even if you decide not to open the old junk drawer, you'll probably just start a new one. Eventually, the new one will look like the old one. The difference is that if you pay attention to what is going in, you will determine what you'll find when you open the new one.

Do you ever wonder why you go looking for those old regrets? If they were any good, you wouldn't have put them in the junk drawer in the first place. You may wonder where that memory is that you haven't thought about in a long time. So you go to the mental junk drawer, looking for it. When you get into a situation, you may remember that there's that bad memory that you've hung onto for a long time. It was in my mental junk drawer all the time. Any experience can trigger an emotion, whether good or bad. You can hear a song or smell a scent, and it can remind you of a time in your life. You may not remember exactly what you were doing, but you do know if it was a good or bad experience.

Minimize all the negative stuff that you store in your mind. When something happens, you want to be able to pull up good memories from your past. If you fill your junk drawer with positive things, then it has meaning and purpose in your life. You want to get to a place in your life where you don't regret yesterday. That is not to say that if you had to do it all over again, you would make the same choices, but you no longer regret the choices you did make, because you accept that you can't change it. No more time, effort, and energy wasted, which you could be using to make a better today.

This is a process that doesn't happen overnight. You cannot modify a lifetime of memories in the blink of an eye. You have to take small steps. You can't swallow an elephant whole. You have to take little bites. Small steps over time will yield big results. When something comes up from your past that makes you feel anything other than good, think about it, and identify what happened. What was the reason that you're feeling like this? What was your role? What could you have done differently to make this particular situation turn out differently? Then, let it go! Don't put it back in the junk drawer.

Maybe you think that if you could go back in time, you would change certain things. You have to understand that everything happens for a reason. Even if you could go back, there might not be anything different that you would have done, because that is where you were then. If someone had told me that all of the trials that I went through in my marriage were to get me to this point, I would not have believed them. Although you may not understand why something is happening now, as the old folk used to say, "by and by" it will be revealed. You have to understand that you did not have the wisdom then that you, hopefully, have now, looking back. This is all part of a journey you're on called life. You make mistakes, and you learn from them. Letting go of your past means not forgetting it, but learning from it, holding onto the good memories, and moving forward to make new memories.

One way to make new memories is to associate with new people. If you're an eagle, hang with eagles; don't be around chickens. People can have a great influence on your ability to accept what is, and let go of what was. You must associate with people who are going to lift you up, and not tear you down. The wrong people around you are like poison. People are in your life for a season, but it is up to you how much of an impact these people have in your life.

Your life is like a window shade. You control how high you want to lift the shade to let people peep inside to see who you are. The higher you lift the window shade of your life, the more opportunity you're giving people to peep inside to criticize or to comfort. That is why it is so important to be selective with the people that you talk to.

You should be seeking balance in your conversations. Don't always dwell on the negative things of life. Everyone has to deal with the stuff of life. Constantly thinking about all of the bad things in your life only brings about more bad things, because that's where your mind is. Be careful about who's in your ear. Who are you listening to? Are you listening to positive people who are motivating you, or are you listening to people who are constantly talking about what you used to be and what you used to do? You don't do what you used to do. If you want a different outcome than what you've got, you have to do things differently. Who are you listening to? Who you listen to will influence how you think, and how you think influences your decisions. Those decisions ultimately influence your actions. Eliminate those negative conversations that come your way. You can tell when someone is coming to you with negative conversation, gossip, etc. You control how much of this type of negativity gets into your ear. Only listen to things that are going to get you to where you want to be.

You'll eventually get to a point in your life when it's time to reach out and help someone else. Your experience and your testimony can be such an encouragement to someone else. When your life gets back on track, help someone else. Share your testimony and your journey. You will begin to understand that what's good for someone else may not be good for you. You will stop comparing yourself to what someone else has and start surrounding yourself with people who are encouraging you and trying to do better. You will start to see things better. The only way to get to that point is to look at yourself and your past relationships. Identify the good, the bad, and the ugly things from your past relationships. This will help you to eliminate certain people from your life without trying to change them to fit into your drama. Everybody has drama in their life. Don't try to make someone else sit in the front row of your movie. And certainly, don't sign up to be a part of someone else's drama.

Have you ever replayed the same mistakes over and over in

your head until you just can't get past your guilt? Or, are you sometimes gripped with the thought of what you should have done? Sometimes we can allow our past to have such a grip on our present that we deny ourselves the benefits waiting in our future.

How to Keep From Living in Your Past

1. Name something from your past that's hard to let go of.

_____

_____

_____

_____

_____

2. If you could do something differently, what would you do?

_____

_____

_____

_____

_____

3. Is there something you can do now to correct it? If so, what? If not, what do you need to do to move on?

_____

_____

_____

_____

_____

_____

How to Deal With Your Past Mistakes

1. Name a mistake from your past that you wish you could change?

_____

_____

_____

_____

_____

_____

2. How has that decision impacted your life?

3. If you hadn't made that mistake, how do you think your life would be different?

4. What can you do to move forward beyond your mistake?

_____

_____

_____

_____

_____

_____

_____

5. How can you own the shame or guilt that you feel from your past mistakes?

_____

_____

_____

_____

_____

_____

How to Let Go

1. How can you tell a new story about your life, concentrating on what you do have and releasing past hurts?

_____

_____

_____

_____

_____

_____

2. What do you have to be grateful and thankful for?

_____

_____

_____

_____

_____

_____

3. What problems does holding onto your past mistakes
    cause you in your current relationships?

_____

_____

_____

_____

_____

_____

_____

4. What are some of the effects on your life of carrying
    around old mistakes (e.g. anger and bitterness, etc.)?

_____

_____

_____

_____

_____

_____

Dealing with Painful Thoughts

1.   What emotions do your past mistakes bring up?

_____

_____

_____

_____

_____

_____

2.   How can you eliminate negative, painful thoughts?

_____

_____

_____

_____

_____

_____

_____

3. What do you need to do to become so grounded in the present that you can look at your past in a different way?

_____

_____

_____

_____

_____

_____

_____

4. What are some small things you can let go of in your mind?

_____

_____

_____

_____

_____

_____

5. What lesson can you learn from your past?

_____

_____

_____

_____

_____

_____

_____

Conclusion

We all have baggage that we bring with us. Some of it is good, and some is not so good. Whether it's good or bad, it directly affects the quality of your life today. Learning how to deal with issues from your past is a key to a successful journey. There are times that you may try to sweep them under the rug, hoping they'll go away, only to have them resurface later on in your life. This book is meant as a guide to help you understand, deal with, and close the chapters of your life that aren't moving you up to a higher level. It is intended to help you get from where you are to where you want to be. Your past is past, and until you come to grips with that, it will be difficult for you to deal with the present!

Blessings to You!!

About the Author

Linda H. Williams

Linda's natural gifts and abilities are teaching, speaking, communicating (both oral and written) and coaching. Linda is motivated to communicate, influence, exhort, and empower the women she interacts with.

Her passion is to help women live their best lives and to reach a higher life. This is accomplished through her motivators: life coach, mentor, facilitator, author, and inspirational speaker. It is Linda's passion to influence women in such a way as to motivate them into positive action.

Linda works tirelessly, providing her services to various women's organizations. She has facilitated support groups for the Cascade House (which is under the auspices of the Y.W.C.A.), the Clayton County Association Against Family Violence, and the Sister Circle for Sisters Empowerment Network. She has also provided inspirational speaking for various women's causes. She provides life skills to the Fayette County Women's Prison system and to community-based programs offered through Community & Housing Initiatives Corporation.

Linda conducts workshops. Recent clients include an engineering consortium, The National Black Women's Life Balance and Wellness Conference, and Sanford-Brown College.

Linda has served as the Director of Women's Programs for Community & Housing Initiatives Corporation and has been a contributing writer to e-magazines for ItsAllAboutWomen. com and SelfGrowth.com.

Linda has served as the Chairperson for the Women's Ministry at the Olivet Church and as the Director of Women's Services for the Olivet Community Development Corporation.

Linda is the Founder and Executive Director of Discover A New Beginning, Inc. Founded in 2005, her organization is committed to the empowerment and restoration of women.

Linda has a BA in English from the State University of New York at Buffalo and is a Certified Life Coach of Life Breakthrough Coaching and Academy.

Find out more about Linda and her Discover a New Beginning Life Coaching Program at www.LindaHWilliams.com.